Integrated Korean
Beginning 2

KLEAR Textbooks in Korean Language

Integrated Korean

Beginning 2

Second Edition

Young-mee Cho   Hyo Sang Lee   Carol Schulz   Ho-min Sohn   Sung-Ock Sohn

University of Hawai'i Press
Honolulu

This textbook series has been developed by the Korean Language Education and Research Center (KLEAR) with the support of the Korea Foundation.

Library of Congress Cataloging-in-Publication Data
Integrated Korean : beginning / Young-mee Cho … [et al.].—2nd ed.
   p. cm.—(KLEAR textbooks in Korean language)
  English and Korean.
  ISBN 978-0-8248-3440-1 (v. 1 : alk. paper)
  1. Korean language—Textbooks for foreign speakers—English.   I. Cho,
Young-mee.
II. Series.
  PL913.I5812 2009
495.7'82421—dc22

                                2009075350

Integrated Korean: Beginning 2, **Second Edition**
ISBN 978-0-8248-3515-6

Illustrations and photos by Sejin Han

Audio files for this volume may be downloaded on the Web in MP3 format at http://www.kleartextbook.com

A set of accompanying audio CDs for this book is also available for purchase. For more information, contact:

Order Department
University of Hawai'i Press
2840 Kolowalu Street
Honolulu, Hawaii 96822
Toll free: 888-847-7377
Outside North America: 808-956-8255

Camera-ready copy has been provided by the authors.

Printed by Data Reproductions, Inc.

FLIP

Contents

Preface to the Second Edition   vii

Objectives   1

Lesson 9   생일 [Birthday]   4
Lesson 10   연구실에서 [At a Professor's Office]   28
Lesson 11   기숙사 생활 [Living in a Dormitory]   52
Lesson 12   가족 [Family]   76
Lesson 13   전화 [On the Telephone]   102
Lesson 14   공항에서 [At the Airport]   128
Lesson 15   쇼핑 [Shopping]   150
Lesson 16   음식점에서 [At a Restaurant]   170
Lesson 17   취미 [Hobbies]   195

Appendices   225
    Appendix 1-1. Copula, Adjective, and Verb Conjugations   225
    Appendix 1-2. Conjugation of Irregular Adjectives and Verbs   229
    Appendix 1-3. The Three Types of Conjugation   237
    Appendix 2. Kinship Terms   238
    Appendix 3. Numbers   239
    Appendix 4. Counters   241

Grammar Index   243
Korean - English Glossary   245
English - Korean Glossary   256

Preface to the Second Edition

The inaugural volumes of *Integrated Korean*, Beginning 1 and 2, of the Korean Language Education & Research Center (KLEAR) appeared in 2000, followed in subsequent years by upper-level (Intermediate, Advanced Intermediate, Advanced, and High Advanced) volumes. The IK series, especially the beginning and intermediate volumes, have attracted a large number of learners of Korean around the world, especially in the United States and other English-speaking countries. Currently, more than seventy universities and colleges are using them for regular classroom instruction. The IK series has been popular particularly because the authors endeavored to develop all volumes in accordance with performance-based principles and methodology—contextualization, learner-centeredness, use of authentic materials, usage-orientedness, balance between acquiring and using skills, and integration of speaking, listening, reading, writing, and culture. Also, grammar points were systematically introduced with simple but adequate explanations and abundant examples and exercises.

The volumes, however, are not free from minor shortcomings that call for improvement. While using the volumes, classroom teachers and students of keen insight, as well as the authors themselves, have noticed such weaknesses here and there. The authors have felt that the volumes should be updated to better reflect the current needs of students. Consequently, at the original authors' recommendation, a revision team was formed, consisting of

Mee-Jeong Park, University of Hawaiʻi at Mānoa (Coordinator)
Joowon Suh, Princeton University
Mary Shin Kim, University of California at Los Angeles
Sang-suk Oh, Harvard University
Hangtae Cho, University of Minnesota

With a strong commitment to offering the best possible learning opportunities, the revision team has painstakingly reorganized and restructured the material in this second edition of the textbook based on feedback received from an extensive survey. This revised edition includes a new layout that more closely mimics the actual classroom environment, making it easier and more intuitive for both teacher and student. Both

Beginning 1 and Beginning 2 now consist of more lessons, but each lesson is more focused, with fewer grammar patterns, and each of these lessons is now divided into two main sections—Conversation 1 and Conversation 2 (each with its own vocabulary list)—followed by Narration. There are more exercises that focus on vocabulary and grammar, with all exercises following our new goal of clarification and intuitiveness.

Each situation/topic-based lesson of the main texts consists of model dialogues, narration, new words and expressions, vocabulary notes, culture, grammar, usage to cover pragmatic uses, and English translation of dialogues. In response to comments from hundreds of students and instructors of the first edition, this new edition features a more attractive two-color design with all new photos and illustrations, additional lessons, and vocabulary exercises.

On behalf of KLEAR and the original authors of IK Beginning 1 and 2, I wholeheartedly thank the revision team for their indefatigable efforts and devotion.

Ho-min Sohn
KLEAR President
April 2010

Objectives

Lesson 9 생일 [Birthday]

Texts	Grammar
Conversation 1 예쁜 모자를 선물 받았어요.	1. Expressing goal or source: N한테/께 vs. N한테서 2. The noun-modifying form [Adj~(으)ㄴ] + N
Conversation 2 할머니 연세가 어떻게 되세요?	3. Honorific expressions 4. The subject honorific ~(으)시 5. The clausal connective ~지만
Narration 돌 잔치	
Culture	**Usage**
나이와 생일 (Age and birthday)	A. Talking about important dates B. Dates, days, and schedules C. Giving/making/sending and receiving D. Organizing a birthday party

Lesson 10 연구실에서 [At a Professor's Office]

Texts	Grammar
Conversation 1 오늘은 시간이 없는데요.	1. The clausal connective ~(으)ㄴ/는데 2. Expressing desire: ~고 싶다/싶어하다 3. The sentence ending ~(으)ㄴ/는데요
Conversation 2 늦어서 죄송합니다.	4. The clausal connective ~어서/아서 (cause) 5. The noun-modifying form [Verb~는] + N
Narration 호주 학생 '마크'	
Culture	**Usage**
서울의 대중 교통 (Public transportation in Seoul) 1. 버스 (Bus) 2. 지하철 (Subway) 3. 택시 (Taxi)	A. Visiting a professor's office: How to start a conversation B. Giving one's biographical information C. Expressing reservations D. Making an apology and giving reasons

Lesson 11 기숙사 생활 [Living in a Dormitory]

Texts	Grammar
Conversation 1 차 한 잔 하실래요?	1. The progressive form ~고 있다 2. Intentional ~(으)ㄹ래요
Conversation 2 연극 보러 갈까요?	3. N(이)나 vs. N밖에 4. Asking someone's opinion: ~(으)ㄹ까요?
Narration 캐나다 학생 '민지'	
Culture	**Usage**
한국의 음악 (Music in Korea)	A. Meeting someone by chance B. Extending, accepting, and declining invitations C. Setting up a get-together

Lesson 12 가족 [Family]

Texts	Grammar
Conversation 1 어디서 오셨어요?	1. The clausal connective ~어서/아서 (sequential) 2. Conjectural ~겠~
Conversation 2 가족 사진이 잘 나왔네요.	3. The sentence ending ~네요 4. Irregular predicates with /ㅎ/ 5. The noun-modifying form [Verb~(으)ㄴ] + N (past)
Narration 가족 사진	
Culture	**Usage**
1. 아름다운 한복 (Beautiful *hanbok*) 2. 호칭 (Extending family terms to other social relations)	A. Talking about family B. Ordinal numbers C. Describing clothes D. Describing colors

Lesson 13 전화 [On the Telephone]

Texts	Grammar
Conversation 1 스티브씨 좀 바꿔 주세요.	1. The benefactive expression ~어/아 주다 2. Expressing obligation or necessity: ~어/아야 되다 3. The sentence ending ~(으)ㄹ게요
Conversation 2 박 교수님 댁이지요?	4. Noun 때문에 5. Intentional ~겠~
Narration 전화 메시지	
Culture	**Usage**
분주한 지하철 (Busy subway)	A. Making telephone calls B. Making an appointment C. Describing illness or pain D. Making a polite request/question

Lesson 14 공항에서 [At the Airport]

Texts	Grammar
Conversation 1 토요일이라서 길이 막히네요.	1. N (이)라서 'because it is N' 2. The negative ~지 못하다
Conversation 2 마중 나왔어요.	3. The adverbial form ~게 4. Negative commands ~지 마세요 5. Irregular predicates in 르
Narration 민지의 편지	
Culture	**Usage**
한국의 종교 (Religions in Korea)	A. Taking a taxi B. Writing letters and postcards

Lesson 15 쇼핑 [Shopping]

Texts	Grammar
Conversation 1 어서 오세요.	1. ~(으)ㄹ 수 있다/없다 'can/cannot' 2. Compound verbs
Conversation 2 이 서점에 자주 오세요?	3. ~(으)면서 'while ~ing' 4. The noun-modifying form [Verb~(으)ㄹ] + N (prospective) 5. The clausal connective ~고 나서
Narration 동대문 시장	
Culture	**Usage**
인사동 (Insa-dong)	A. Asking about prices; buying things B. Expressing frequency

Lesson 16 음식점에서 [At a Restaurant]

Texts	Grammar
Conversation 1 냉면 먹어 봤어요?	1. ~어/아 보다 'try doing' 2. The nominalizer ~기 3. The clausal connective ~기 때문에 (reason)
Conversation 2 육개장이 맵지 않아요?	4. Giving and offering: ~어/아 드리다 5. Negation: ~지 않다
Narration 점심 식사	
Culture	**Usage**
음식 문화 (Food culture)	A. Making suggestions B. Ordering food C. Describing tastes

Lesson 17 취미 [Hobbies]

Texts	Grammar
Conversation 1 취미가 뭐예요?	1. (An act of) ~ing: ~는 것 2. The conditional ~(으)면 'if, when' 3. The comparative 보다 (더) 'more than'
Conversation 2 운동 좋아하세요?	4. N 때 'at the time of N'; ~(으)ㄹ 때 'when' 5. ~(으)ㄹ 줄 알다/모르다 'know/not know how to'
Narration 취미가 다른 두 사람	
Culture	**Usage**
축구, 야구, 씨름, 그리고 태권도 (Soccer, baseball, Ssirŭm, and Taekwondo)	A. Talking about favorite activities B. Describing feelings

9과 생일 [Birthday]

Conversation 1	예쁜 모자를 선물 받았어요.

스티브: 리사 씨, 지난 주말에 뭐 했어요?

리사: 토요일이 제 생일이었어요.

그래서 생일 파티 했어요.

스티브: 아, 그랬어요? 축하해요.

리사: 고마워요.

스티브: 생일 선물 많이 받았어요?

리사: 네, 친구들한테서[G9.1] 많이 받았어요.

스티브: 무슨 선물 받았어요?

리사: 책하고 예쁜[G9.2] 모자를 받았어요.

스티브 씨 생일은 언제예요?

스티브: 제 생일은 6월 27일이에요.

NEW WORDS

NOUN		VERB	
건물	building	보내다	② to send
돈	money	축하하다	to congratulate
돌	the first birthday	**ADJECTIVE**	
며칠	what date; a few days	길다	to be long
모자	cap, hat	짧다	to be short
번호	number		
올해	this year	**PARTICLE**	
이메일	e-mail	께 *hon.*	to (a person)
잔치	feast, party	와/과	and (joins nouns)
카드	card	한테	to (a person or an animal; colloquial form)
편지	letter		
SUFFIX		한테서	from (a person or an animal; colloquial form)
~(으)ㄴ	noun modifying form		

NEW EXPRESSIONS

1. In Korean, dates are expressed in Sino-Korean numbers (e.g., 일, 이, 삼, 사, 오 . . .) in the order of year-month-day.

오늘은 며칠이에요?   What day of the month is it today?
오늘은 2013년 12월 29일이에요.   Today is December 29, 2013.

2. Months of the year:

1월	January	7월	July
2월	February	8월	August
3월	March	9월	September
4월	April	10월(시월)	October
5월	May	11월	November
6월 (유월)	June	12월	December

3. Days of the month:

1일	the first	12일	the twelfth
2일	the second	20일	the twentieth
3일	the third	31일	the thirty-first

Exercises

1. Practice reading the following dates.

(1)	January 1st	(2)	April 5th
(3)	June 6th	(4)	August 17th
(5)	October 3rd	(6)	December 21st

2. Fill in the blanks with your own information.

(1)   제 생일은 _____월 _____일이에요.

(2)   지난 크리스마스에 _____한테서 _____을/를 받았어요.

(3)   A: 오늘 며칠이에요?

       B: _____월 _____일이에요.

(4)   친구한테 _____을/를 선물할 거예요.

GRAMMAR

G9.1	Expressing goal or source : N한테/께 vs. N한테서

Examples

[Person]한테/께 'to (a person)'

(1)   유미: 리사 씨, 언니**한테** 이메일 자주 보내세요?

       리사: 아니요, 자주 못 보내요.

             유미 씨는 부모님**께** 편지 자주 하세요?

       유미: 네, 자주 해요.

(2)   어제는 리사 생일이었어요.

       그래서 리사**한테** 꽃과 카드를 주었어요.

[Person]한테서 'from (a person)'

    (3)   소피아: 리사 씨, 올해 생일 선물 많이 받았어요?
                리사: 꽃하고 책을 받았어요.
                소피아: 누구**한테서** 책을 받았어요?
                리사: 마이클**한테서** 받았어요.

    (4)   스티브: 마이클 씨, 리사**한테서** 전화 왔어요.
                마이클: 네, 고마워요.

[Place]에 'to (a place)'

    (5)   제니: 마이클 씨, 서울**에** 며칠에 가요?
                마이클: 10월 13일에 가요.

    (6)   스티브: 소피아 씨, 홍콩**에** 전화 자주 하세요?
                소피아: 네, 자주 해요.

[Place]에서 'from (a place)'

    (7)   제니: 서울**에서** 편지가 왔어요.

    (8)   스티브: 마이클 씨, 집**에서** 전화 왔어요.
                마이클: 누구예요?
                스티브: 마이클 씨 동생이에요.

Notes

1. The particle 한테 is used with 'giving or sending' verbs while 한테서 is used with 'receiving' verbs.

'giving or sending' type	'receiving' type
N한테 선물(을) 하다/주다	N한테서 선물(을) 받다
N한테 전화(를) 하다	N한테서 전화(를) 받다/ 전화(가) 오다
N한테 편지(를) 보내다	N한테서 편지(를) 받다/ 편지(가) 오다
N한테 애기(를) 하다	N한테서 애기(를) 듣다

2. When the recipient is a respected senior (e.g., 부모님 and 선생님), the honorific particle 께 should be used instead of 한테, as in (1).

3. The particle 도 can be added after 한테 or 한테서 to indicate 'also, too'.

어제 마이클한테 전화 했어요. 그리고 리사한테도 전화 했어요.
마이클한테서 이메일이 왔어요. 그리고 유미한테서도 왔어요.

4. While 한테 and 한테서 are used with persons, 에 and 에서 are used with places. The particles 에 (G5.1) and 에서 express 'to (a place)' and 'from (a place)' respectively as in (5)~(8).

Exercises

1. Describe the pictures as shown in (1).

(1)

메리/제임스   메리가 제임스한테 전화 번호를 주었어요.

(2)

유미/리사   유미<s>는</s>가 리사 한테 책을 줘요
<s>유미한테</s>

(3)

스티브/유미   스티브<s>는</s>가 유미한테 꽃을 줘요

(4)

리사/김 선생님   김 선생님께서 리사한테서 전화를 받으셨어요

2. Fill in the blanks with the proper particles, provided in the box below.

께	에	에서	한테	한테서

(1)   리사가 마이클 한테____ 전화를 했어요.

(2)   유미는 생일에 스티브 한테서____ 카드를 받았어요.

(3)   소피아는 로스앤젤레스 에____ 전화했어요.

(4)   민지는 조카('nephew') 돌 잔치 에____ 꽃을 보냈어요

(5)   어제 오빠 한테서____ 전화가 왔어요.

(6)   부모님 께____ 편지 자주 쓰세요?

(7)   라디오 ('radio') 에서____ 음악을 들었어요.

(8)   스티브가 크리스마스에 형 한테서____ 돈을 받았어요.

G9.2   The noun-modifying form [Adj~(으)ㄴ] + N

Examples

(1)   우체국은 **큰** 건물 안에 있어요.

(2)   리사는 백화점에서 **좋은** 옷을 샀어요.

(3)   스티브는 시청에서 **가까운** 아파트에 살아요.

(4)   교회 옆에 작고 **예쁜** 꽃집이 있습니다.

Notes

1. ~(으)ㄴ occurs with adjectives and is used to modify nouns, as in 큰 집 'big house'.

Examples of adjective stems that end in vowels:

Adjective stem + ㄴ	
Dictionary form	Noun-modifying form
크다 to be big	큰 big
싸다 to be inexpensive	싼 inexpensive
예쁘다 to be pretty	예쁜 pretty

Examples of adjective stems that end in consonants:

Adjective stem + 은	
Dictionary form	Noun-modifying form
좋다 to be good	좋은 good
많다 to be many	많은 plentiful
작다 to be small	작은 small

2. Noun-modifying forms of the irregular predicates in /ㅂ/ and /ㄹ/:

Examples of irregular adjectives in /ㅂ/:

If /ㅂ/ is at the end of the adjective stem, it is changed to 우 before a vowel (G6.2).

가깝 + 은 → 가까우 + 은 → 가까우 + ㄴ → 가까운

Dictionary form	Noun-modifying form
가깝다 to be close, near	가까운 집
춥다 to be cold	추운 날씨
어렵다 to be difficult	어려운 시험
쉽다 to be easy	쉬운 숙제

Examples of regular adjectives in /ㅂ/:

Dictionary form	Noun-modifying form
좁다 to be narrow	좁은 방
짧다 to be short	짧은 머리 ('hair')

Examples of irregular adjectives in /ㄹ/:

When an adjective stem ending in /ㄹ/ is followed by /ㄴ/, /ㅂ/, or /ㅅ/, the final /ㄹ/ is omitted (G8.5). In the following example, the syllable 은 is shortened to ㄴ, and then, the adjective stem-final /ㄹ/ is deleted because of the following /ㄴ/.

멀 + 은 → 멀 + ㄴ → 머 + ㄴ → 먼

Dictionary form		Noun-modifying form
멀다	to be far	먼 거리 ('distance')
길다	to be long	긴 머리

3. Adjectives 있다/ 없다 take ~는 instead of ~(으)ㄴ.

Dictionary form		Noun-modifying form	
재미있다	to be interesting, fun	재미있는	interesting
맛없다	to not be tasty	맛없는	bad-tasting

4. When you use more than one adjective, the adjectives are connected with ~고 'and', and only the last adjective takes the noun-modifying form, as in 비싸고 좋은 옷 'expensive and nice clothes', 싸고 맛있는 음식 'cheap and tasty food', and 깨끗하고 넓은 집 'clean and spacious house'.

Exercises

1. Fill in the blanks with appropriate noun-modifying forms.

    (1) _____ 나라

    (2) _____ 대학교

    (3) _____ 영화

    (4) _____ 동네

2. Translate the following sentences into Korean.

(1)   Lisa is a *good* <u>student</u>.

리사는 좋은 학생이에요.

(2)   I like *large* <u>bags</u>.

큰 가방을 좋아해요

(3)   I bought this present at a *nearby* <u>department store</u>.

가까운 백화점 에서 샀어요

(4)   I bought a *small* and *pretty* <u>watch</u>.

작고 예쁜 시계를 샀어요

(5)   I live in a *quiet* and *clean* <u>apartment</u>.

저는 깨끗하고 조용한 아파트에서 살아요

Conversation 2 | 할머니 연세가 어떻게 되세요?

마크: 제니 씨, 주말에 바빴어요?

제니: 네, 일요일이 할머니 생신[G9.3]이었어요.

그래서 가족들하고 같이 저녁을 먹었어요.

마크: 아, 그랬어요?

제니: 네, 오래간만에 즐거운 시간을 보냈어요.

할머니께서 아주 좋아하셨어요.[G9.4]

마크: 할머니께 선물 드렸어요?

제니: 스웨터하고 장갑을 드렸어요.

마크: 할머니 연세가 어떻게 되세요?

제니: 올해 일흔 다섯이세요.

마크: 할머니께서 건강하세요?

제니: 네, 연세는 많으시지만[G9.5] 아주 건강하세요.

NEW WORDS

NOUN		VERB	
가족	family	돌아가시다 *hon.*	to pass away
나이	age	드리다 *hum.*	to give (=주다 *plain*)
딸	daughter	드시다 *hon.*	to eat (=먹다 *plain*)
댁 *hon.*	home, house (=집 *plain*)	주무시다 *hon.*	to sleep (=자다 *plain*)
사진	photo, picture	죽다	to die
생신 *hon.*	birthday (=생일 *plain*)	찍다	to take (a photo)
성함 *hon.*	name (=이름 *plain*)	**ADJECTIVE**	
스웨터	sweater	건강하다	to be healthy
아들	son	즐겁다	to be joyful
연세 *hon.*	age	**ADVERB**	
작년	last year	모두	all
장갑	gloves	**PARTICLE**	
할머니	grandmother	께서 *hon.*	subject particle
할아버지	grandfather		(=이/가 *plain*)
COUNTER		**SUFFIX**	
살	years old	~(으)시	subject honorifics
분 *hon.*	people (=명 *plain*)		

NEW EXPRESSIONS

1. 께 is the honorific counterpart of 한테. It is used for highly respected seniors: for example, parents, grandparents, or teachers.

2. 께서 is the honorific counterpart of the subject particle 이/가, not of 한테서 'from (a person)'. The honorific form of 한테서 is also 께 as in 부모님께 편지를 받았어요.

3. 보내다 'to send' has an additional meaning, 'to spend time', as in 가족들하고 즐거운 시간을 보냈어요 (Lesson 7, Conv. 2).

4. 어떻게 되세요? is a polite idiomatic expression that is the equivalent to 뭐예요? 언제예요? 몇이에요? (what is . . . , when is . . . , how many/much is . . .). For example, it would be more appropriate to use the expression 성함이 어떻게 되세요? than 이름이 뭐예요? when addressing seniors or new acquaintances.

Exercise

Connect the corresponding words.

선물   •   • 드리다

생일   •   • 찍다

시간   •   • 보내다

사진   •   • 축하하다

GRAMMAR

G9.3   Honorific expressions

Examples

(1)   동생이 책을 읽어요.   My younger sibling is reading
                                          a book.

       아버지**께서** 책을 읽**으세**요.   My father is reading a book.
                                          (subject honorific)

(2)   제 동생 나이는 열 여덟 살이에요.   My younger sibling is 18
                                          years old.

       저희 할머니 **연세**는   My grandmother is 72 years
       일흔 둘**이세**요.   old. (subject honorific)

(3)   우리 집 개는 작년에 죽었습니다.
       저희 할아버지**께서** 작년에 **돌아가셨**습니다.

Notes

Korean is a language whose honorific patterns are highly systematic.
Honorific forms appear in hierarchical address/reference terms and titles,
some commonly used nouns and verbs, the pronoun system, particles,
and verb suffixes. Sentences in Korean can hardly be composed without
knowledge of one's social relationships to the listener or referent in terms
of age, social status, and kinship. The following table is a summary of
honorific forms.

		Plain	Honorific	Humble
Nouns	age	나이	연세	
	name	이름	성함	
	birthday	생일	생신	
	words	말	말씀	
	house	집	댁	
	meal	밥	진지	
	counter for people	사람/명	분	
Pronouns	he/she	이/그/저 사람	이/그/저 분	
	I	나는/내가		저는/제가
	my	내		제
	we/our	우리		저희
Verbs	to see/meet someone	보다/만나다	보시다/만나시다	뵙다
	to be	있다	계시다	
	to die	죽다	돌아가시다	
	to be well, fine	잘 있다	안녕하시다	
	to sleep	자다	주무시다	
	to eat	먹다/들다	잡수시다/드시다	
	to give	주다	주시다	드리다
	to speak	말하다	말씀하시다	말씀드리다
Particles	subject	이/가	께서	
	topic	은/는	께서는	
	goal	한테/에게	께	
	source	한테서/에게서	께	
Suffixes	professor	교수	교수님	
	parents	부모	부모님	
	teacher	선생	선생님	

Subject honorific forms: [N께서 . . . V/Adj~(으)시]

The particle 께서 is the honorific counterpart of the subject particle 이/가.
The subject honorific suffix ~(으)시 is used when the subject—a social
or familial superior, a distant peer, or a stranger—must be referred or
spoken to with respect.

While ~(으)시 must be used when the subject is honored, use of 께서 is not obligatory. When it is used, it shows special respect toward the subject of the sentence.

내 동생이 도서관에 가요.　　vs.　　저희 할머니께서 집에 가세요.

When talking about your grandparents, parents, or any elders, the subject honorific particle 께서 is used in addition to the subject honorific suffix ~(으)시 to pay respect to them. When talking about your close friends or younger siblings, on the other hand, ~(으)시 is not allowed. Note further that the presence of ~어요/아요 or ~습/ㅂ니다 shows respect to the listener.

　　Some nouns and verbs have honorific counterparts such as 나이/연세, 이름/성함, 딸/따님, 아들/아드님, 자다/주무시다, 먹다/드시다 as shown in the following example sentences.

할아버지께서는 연세가 많으세요.	My grandfather is old.
	(lit. My grandfather has much age.)
선생님, 따님은 어디에 계세요?	Sir, where is your daughter?
아버지께서 지금 주무십니다.	My father is sleeping now.

Exercise

Choose the appropriate forms within the [ ] and circle them.

(1)　　Server:　　[모두 몇 분이세요? /모두 몇 사람이에요?]

　　　　Customer:　　[세 분이에요 /세 사람이에요.]

(2)　　할머니께서 동생한테 책을 [주었어요/주셨어요/드렸어요.]

(3)　　저희 부모님께서는 [연세가 많으세요/나이가 많으세요.]

(4)　　아버지, 저 약국에 [갑니다/가십니다/가실 거예요.]

(5)　　할아버지, 저기 동생이 [와요/오세요/오십니다.]

G9.4 The subject honorific ~(으)시

Examples

(1) 마이클: 어, 제니 씨. 요즘 어떻게 지내**세**요?
    제니: 잘 지내요. 마이클 씨, 이번 학기에도 심리학
             들**으세**요?
    마이클: 아니요, 이번 학기에는 안 들어요.

(2) 마크: 스티브 씨 어디서 오**셨**어요?
    스티브: 저는 미국 보스톤에서 왔어요.

(3) 마크: 저어, 이번 학기에 한국어를 누가 가르치**십**니까?
    현우: 이민수 선생님께서 가르치**십**니다.

(4) 마크: 이민수 선생님 계**십**니까?
    현우: 지금 안 **계세**요.

Notes

1. ~(으)시 is added to a predicate stem to express the speaker's respect toward the subject of the sentence.

2. ~(으)시 is not a sentence-final suffix, and therefore it is always followed by other types of suffixes as in 읽으시었습니다 [읽+으시+었+습니다].

	Plain		Subject honorific	
	Non-past	Past	Non-past	Past
Polite	~어/아요	~었/았어요	~(으)세요	~(으)셨어요
Deferential	~습/ㅂ니다	~었/았습니다	~(으)십니다	~(으)셨습니다

Examples

	Plain		Subject Honorific	
	Non-past	Past	Non-past	Past
Polite	가요 읽어요	갔어요 읽었어요	가세요 읽으세요	가셨어요 읽으셨어요
Deferential	갑니다 읽습니다	갔습니다 읽었습니다	가십니다 읽으십니다	가셨습니다 읽으셨습니다

3. ~(으)시 is already part of some honorific predicates, as in example (4).

	Non-past	Past
Polite	계세요	계셨어요
Deferential	계십니다	계셨습니다

Exercise

Fill in the blanks with appropriate honorific forms of the verb. Be consistent with the tense and the speech style in the conversation.

(1) 마크: 스티브 씨, 어디서 <u>오셨어요</u> (오다)?

    스티브:저는 미국 보스톤에서 왔어요.

(2) A: 김 선생님 ___계세요___ (계시다)? ~~계셔~~ 계십니까

    B: 지금 안 ~~계십니다~~ (계시다).

       수업에 ___가셨어요___ (가다).

(3) A: 이 지도 어느 서점에서 ___사셨어요___ (사다)?

    B: 동네 서점에서 샀어요.

(4) 마크: 선생님, 점심 ___드셨어요___ (드시다)?

    선생님:아니요, 아직 안 먹었어요.

(5) 지난 학기에 몇 과목 ___들으셨어요___(듣다)?

    이번 학기에는 몇 과목 ___들으세요___ (듣다)?   들으세요

    다음 학기에는 몇 과목 ___들으실거예요___(듣다)?

G9.5   The clausal connective ~지만

Examples

(1)   저는 여행은 자주 하**지만**   I travel often but don't take
        사진은 안 찍어요.   pictures.

(2)   나는 편지를 자주 쓰**지만**   I write letters often,
        내 친구는 자주 안 써요.   but my friend does not.

(3)   A: 테니스 좋아하세요?
        B: 좋아하**지만** 자주 못 쳐요.

Notes

1. ~지만 is equivalent to "but" or "although" in English. Remember that with ~고 it is more natural not to express tense in the first clause, but to rely on the second clause to furnish it. This is not the case with ~지만, where both clauses in the sentence must indicate the tense. For example:

쇼핑을 하고 친구를 만났어요. (no tense indicated in first clause)
생일 파티에는 못 **갔**지만 선물은 샀어요. (tense indicated in first clause)

Exercises

1. Connect the clauses in each sentence using the ending ~지만. Change the verb to the past tense if necessary.

(1)   이 시계는 조금 (비싸다) 비싸지만 아주 좋아요.

(2)   미국은 겨울 방학은 (짧다) _____ 여름 방학은
        길어요.

(3)   공부는 (하다) _____ 시험을 못 봤어요.

(4)   마크는 어제 (바쁘다) _____ 친구 파티에 갔어요.

(5)   다음 월요일이 크리스마스(이다) _____ 일을 해요.

(6)   형은 한국에서 (살다) _____ 저는 미국에서 살아요.

2. Use ~지만 to make a complex sentence by changing the verb and adding an appropriate main clause as in the example.

(1)   한국은 날씨가 참 좋아요.

한국은 날씨가 참 좋지만 겨울이 좀 추워요.

(2)   주말이 좋아요.

주말이 좋지만 재미 없어요

(3)   내 여동생은 전공이 컴퓨터예요.

내 여동생은 전공이 컴퓨터지만 정치학을 좋아해요

(4)   우리 가족은 미국에서 살아요.

우리 가족은 미국에서 살지만 한국에 계세요

(5)   서울에는 사람이 아주 많아요.

더 ← more

서울에는 사람이 아주 많지만 미국이 더 많아요

(6)   작년 크리스마스에는 선물을 많이 받았어요.

작년 크리스마스에는 선물을 많이 받았지만

이번 크리스마스에는 선물을 많이 안 받았어요

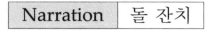

한국에서는 한 살에 돌 잔치를 합니다. 지난 토요일이
한국어 선생님 딸 돌이었습니다. 그래서 저는 반
친구들하고 같이 선생님 댁에 갔습니다. 돌 잔치에서
재미있는 일[1]이 많았습니다. 상[2] 위에 돈, 연필, 실[3]이
있었습니다. 돈은 부자[4]를 뜻하고[5] 연필은 공부를 뜻하고
실은 건강을 뜻합니다. 선생님 딸은 연필을 잡았습니다[6].
한국에서는 보통 돌에 아이[7]한테 금반지[8]를 선물합니다.
그래서 저와 친구들도 금반지를 선물했습니다. 사진도
많이 찍었습니다. 즐거운 돌 잔치였습니다.

1. 일: event   2. 상: table
3. 실: thread   4. 부자: a wealthy person
5. 뜻하다: to mean, to signify   6. 잡다: to catch, to grab
7. 아이: child, kid   8. 금반지: gold ring

Exercises

1. Read the narration and answer the following questions using the deferential ending ~습니다 or ㅂ니다.

(1) 돌 잔치는 무엇입니까?

(2) 누구의 돌 잔치가 있었습니까?

(3) 돌 잔치에 누구하고 같이 갔습니까?

(4) 실과 돈은 무엇을 뜻합니까?

(5) 한국에서는 보통 돌에 무슨 선물을 합니까?

(6) 한국의 돌 잔치는 뭐가 재미있습니까?

2. Fill in the blanks with the appropriate words from the box below.

보통	큰	많이	재미있는
같이	그래서	지난	즐거운

한국에서는 한 살에 돌 잔치를 합니다. _____ 토요일이 한국어 선생님 딸 돌이었습니다. _____ 저는 반 친구들하고 _____ 선생님 댁에 갔습니다. 돌 잔치에서 _____ 일이 많았습니다. 상 위에 돈, 연필, 실 등이 있었습니다. 돈은 부자를 뜻하고 연필은 공부를 뜻하고 실은 건강을 뜻합니다. 선생님 딸은 연필을 잡았습니다. 한국에서는 _____ 돌에 아이한테 금반지를 선물합니다. 그래서 저와 친구들도 금반지를 선물했습니다. 사진도 _____ 찍었습니다. _____ 돌 잔치였습니다.

CULTURE

나이와 생일 (Age and birthday)

Many people get confused with the way Koreans calculate age. It is easy, however, if you keep two things in mind. First, you are one year old the moment you are born. Second, you become a year older not on your birthday but on New Year's Day. This makes a baby born on December 31 two years old the next day after her birth, on New Year's Day.

There are two distinctive birthdays that Koreans celebrate in special ways: 돌 and 환갑. 돌 is the first birthday after your birth; 환갑 is the sixty-first birthday, when the exact same Chinese zodiacal combination comes around for the first time after your birth. They became special birthdays because in the past not many babies made it to their 돌 and not many people lived up to sixty years.

An interesting tradition of 돌 is 돌잡이. Such items as money, rice, books, pencils, thread, a microphone, and so on are arranged on a table for the baby to pick up. It is believed that the item the baby picks up foretells the baby's future. Money and rice are interpreted as a wealthy life, books and pencils as academic success, thread as a long and healthy life, and the microphone as a promising career in the entertainment business. On 환갑, children honor their parents with a large feast and much merrymaking. They show their respect to their parents by bowing on the ground in the order of age. Close relatives are also invited to join the ceremony, to show their respect, and to give presents.

USAGE

A. Talking about important dates

[Exercise] Ask your partner about the following dates.

(1)	today	A:	오늘이 며칠이에요?
		B:	<u>오늘은 12월 12일이에요.</u>

(2)   your birthday

(3)   Valentine's Day

(4)   Independence Day

(5)　　　Thanksgiving

(6)　　　Christmas

B. Dates, days, and schedules

December 2014						
일요일	월요일	화요일	수요일	목요일	금요일	토요일
	3:00 p.m. 한국어 랩 1	2	Today 3	4	5	3:30 p.m. 농구시합: ＿＿＿ vs. UCLA 6
7	3:00 p.m. 한국어 랩 8	9:00 a.m. 한국어 복습 9	10	9:00 a.m. 한국어 오럴테스트 11	12	1:30 p.m. 농구시합: ＿＿＿vs. Michigan 13
14	8-10 a.m. 한국어 Final exam 15	16	12:30 p.m. 경제학 Final exam 17	Semester ends 18	19	20
21	22	23	24	*Christmas Day* 25	26	11:00 a.m. to Boston 27

(1)　　　오늘은 며칠이에요?　<u>오늘은 12월 3일이에요.</u>

(2)　　　한국어 랩은 무슨 요일에 있어요? 몇 시에 있어요?

(3)　　　한국어 복습('review')은 언제 해요?

(4)　　　15일에는 무슨 시험이 있어요? 시험이 몇 시간 걸려요?

(5)　　　다음 주에는 누가 농구시합('basketball game')을 해요?
　　　　　몇 시에 해요?

(6)　　　경제학 시험은 언제예요?

(7)　　　이번 학기는 며칠에 끝나요 ('to end')?

(8)　　　보스톤에는 언제 가요?

(9)　　　올해 크리스마스는 무슨 요일이에요?

(10)　　내년은 몇 년이에요?

C. Giving/making/sending and receiving

'giving or sending'	'receiving'
N한테 선물(을) 하다/주다/드리다	N한테서 선물(을) 받다
N한테 전화(를) 하다/걸다/드리다	N한테서 전화(를) 받다
N한테 편지(를) 쓰다/보내다	N한테서 편지(를) 받다
N한테 이메일(을) 하다/보내다	N한테서 이메일(을) 받다

[Exercise] Give a description in answer to the following questions.

(1)   생일에 무슨 선물을 받았어요?

(2)   이번 토요일이 친구 생일이에요. 무슨 선물을 줄 거예요?

(3)   누구한테 자주 전화하세요?

(4)   선생님께 언제 전화 드렸어요?

(5)   부모님한테서 언제 전화 받았어요?

(6)   누구한테 크리스마스 카드를 보낼 거예요?

(7)   작년에 누구한테서 크리스마스 카드를 받았어요?

(8)   부모님께 편지 자주 쓰세요?

D. Organizing a birthday party

[Exercise] You are organizing a birthday party. Form groups of three
or four. Each group prepares for the birthday party of one of their own.
Include some of the following:

(1)   Whose birthday it is

(2)   Date, time, and place of the party

(3)   What to include in the invitation

(4)   Deciding on birthday presents

(5)   Things to bring for the party

(6)   Sending out thank-you notes

Lesson 9 - Birthday

CONVERSATION 1: I received a pretty hat.

Steve: Lisa, what did you do last weekend?
Lisa: Saturday was my birthday. So I had a birthday party.
Steve: Oh, really? Happy birthday!
Lisa: Thank you.
Steve: Did you receive a lot of gifts?
Lisa: Yes, a lot from my friends.
Steve: What kinds of gifts did you receive?
Lisa: I received a book and a pretty hat. Steve, when is your birthday?
Steve: My birthday is June 27th.

CONVERSATION 2: How old is your grandmother?

Mark: Jenny, did you have a busy weekend?
Jenny: Yes, it was my grandmother's birthday. So we had a family dinner.
Mark: Oh, really?
Jenny: Yes, it's been a while since we had such a great time. My grandmother enjoyed it a lot.
Mark: Did you get her a gift?
Jenny: I gave her a sweater and a pair of gloves.
Mark: How old is your grandmother?
Jenny: She's seventy-five years old.
Mark: Is she healthy?
Jenny: Yes, she's very healthy for her age.

NARRATION: 'First birthday' party

In Korea, people celebrate *tol*, the first birthday. Last Saturday was the first birthday of my Korean teacher's daughter. So my classmates and I went to her *tol* party. The party was full of fun. They put money, a pencil, and a ball of thread on a table. The money symbolizes wealth, the pencil symbolizes academic success, and the thread symbolizes a long, healthy life. The teacher's daughter grabbed the pencil. In Korea, it is customary to give a gold ring as a gift to the one-year-old. My classmates and I gave her a gold ring as a present, too. We also took many photos. It was a fun *tol* party.

10과 연구실에서 [At a Professor's Office]

| Conversation 1 | 오늘은 시간이 없는데요. |

(Mark introduces himself to Professor Park and makes an arrangement to take the Korean placement test.)

마크: 안녕하세요, 교수님.

교수님: 네, 어떻게 오셨어요?

마크: 제 이름은 마크 스미스입니다.
한국 문화를 전공하는데[G10.1] 이번 학기에
한국어 수업을 듣고 싶습니다.[G10.2]

교수님: 아, 그래요? 한국어를 얼마 동안 배웠어요?

마크: 시드니 대학교에서 일 년 동안 배웠습니다.

교수님: 그럼 오늘 오후에 한국어 시험을 보세요.

마크: 죄송하지만 오늘은 시간이 없는데요.[G10.3]

교수님: 그럼 내일 아침 9시에 시험을 보러 오세요.

마크: 네. 그럼 내일 뵙겠습니다.

신 경과학 - neuroscience

실례 합니다

죄송하지안

부지런하다 → to be hard working

NEW WORDS

NOUN		ADJECTIVE	
교수님	professor	싶다	to want to
동안	during, for	죄송하다	to be sorry
문화	culture	**ADVERB**	
밖	outside	그냥	just, without any special reason
시드니	Sydney		
연구실	professor's office	굉장히	very much
택시	taxi	일찍	early
호주	Australia	**SUFFIX**	
VERB		~(으)ㄴ데/는데	clausal connective
놀다	to play; to not work	~(으)ㄴ데요/ 는데요	a polite sentence ending for background information
시작하다	to begin		

NEW EXPRESSIONS

다니다 → to (frequently) attend

거의 - almost

1. 얼마 'how much', when used with 동안 'during' as in 얼마 동안, means 'for how long'. 동안 in 일 년 동안 'for one year' and 여름 방학 동안 'during the summer break' indicates a duration or period of time. 동안 can be omitted in some contexts, as in 한국어를 일 년 (동안) 배웠습니다 'I studied Korean for one year'.

2.　　A:　　전공이 뭐예요? / 뭐 전공하세요?　　What is your major?
　　　　B:　　심리학(전공)이에요. /　　　　　　　I major in psychology.
　　　　　　심리학을 전공해요.

3. The verb 뵙다 in 내일 뵙겠습니다 'I will see you tomorrow' is the humble form of the verb 보다 'to see' (see G9.3).

Exercises

1. Complete the words by filling in the blanks.

　　　oriental studies:　(동양)학　　　economics:　　　(　　　)학

　　　biology:　　　　(　　　)학　　　Korean studies:　(　　　)학

　　　psychology:　　(　　　)학　　　political science:　(　　　)학

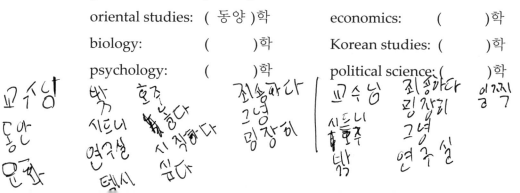

2. Ask your classmates the following questions.

> A: (한국어, 일본어, 중국어, 테니스, 수영) 얼마 동안 배웠어요?
>
> B: _____동안 배웠어요.

GRAMMAR

| G10.1 | The clausal connective ~(으)ㄴ데/는데 |

Examples

(1)   어제 샌디한테 전화**했는데**
　　　집에 없었어요.

I called Sandy yesterday,
but she was not home.

(2)   A: 날씨가 좋**은데**
　　　　　　집에 있을 거예요?
　　　B: 네, 집에 있을 거예요.

The weather is nice; are you
going to stay at home?
Yes, I'm going to stay at
home.

(3)   옷이 예**쁜데** 너무 비싸요.

The clothes are pretty but
too expensive.

(4)   시간이 없**는데** 택시를 타세요.

You are running out of time;
take a taxi.

Notes

1. The main function of ~(으)ㄴ데/는데 is to provide background
information about the situation in the main clause. The pattern ~(으)ㄴ데/
는데 can be used in the following contexts:

   a. to give common background information to be shared between a
      speaker and a listener (examples (1) and (2));

   b. to contrast two clauses (example (3));

   c. to justify a request or proposal (example (4)).

2. ~는데 and ~(으)ㄴ데 alternate as follows:

	~는데		~(으)ㄴ데
a.	Verbs	d.	Adjectives
b.	Past tense	e.	Copula
c.	Existential 있/없		

In the past tense, ~었/았 occurs before the form ~는데. The following table shows the conjugation patterns.

The suffix ~는데

a-b. Verbs/Past tense

Dictionary form		Non-past	Past
가다	to go	가는데	갔는데
먹다	to eat	먹는데	먹었는데
알다	to know	아는데	알았는데
듣다	to listen	듣는데	들었는데

c. 있다/없다

Dictionary form		Non-past	Past
있다	to be, exist	있는데	있었는데
없다	not to be, exist	없는데	없었는데

The suffix ~(으)ㄴ데

d. Adjectives

Dictionary form		Non-past	Past
예쁘다	to be pretty	예쁜데	예뻤는데
좋다	to be good	좋은데	좋았는데
멀다	to be far	먼데	멀었는데
춥다	to be cold	추운데	추웠는데

e. The copula N~이다, N~아니다

Dictionary form	Non-past	Past
학생이다 to be a student	학생인데	학생이었는데
교수이다 to be a professor	교수인데	교수였는데
학생(이) 아니다 not to be . . .	학생(이) 아닌데	학생(이) 아니었는데

Exercise

Combine each pair of sentences using the correct form of ~(으)ㄴ데/는데.

(1)   한국어를 배워요. / 재미있어요.
      [배우는데]

(2)   마크는 호주 사람이에요. / 한국어를 굉장히 잘 해요.
      [사람인데]

(3)   경제학 수업은 재미있어요. / 숙제가 많아요.
      [있는데]

(4)   기숙사에 살아요. / 방이 좁아요.   *[사 는 데]*

(5)   어제 공부 많이 했어요. / 오늘 시험이 없어요.
      [했는데]

(6)   우리 학교 캠퍼스는 예뻐요. / 너무 작아요.
      [예쁜데]

G10.2 Expressing desire: ~고 싶다/ 싶어하다

Examples

(1)   마크: 이번 주말에 뭐 하고 **싶어요**?   What do you want to
                                      do this weekend?

      스티브: 수영하러 가고 **싶어요**.   I want to go
                                      swimming.

(2)   유미는 한국 영화를 보고 **싶어해요**.   Yumi wants to watch
                                      a Korean movie.

(3)   A: 내일 어디 가고 **싶으세요**?   Where do you want
                                      to go tomorrow?

      B: 그냥 집에 있고 **싶어요**.   I just want to stay
                                      home.

(4)   올해에는 운동을 시작하고 **싶었는데** 못 했어요.

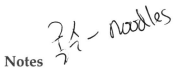

Notes
광심 있다

[Verb~고 싶다] expresses the speaker's desire or, in questions, the listener's desire. The desire or wish of a third person is indicated by ~고 싶어하다 (lit. someone shows signs of wanting).

저는 컴퓨터를 사고 싶어요.   I want to buy a computer.
소피아도 컴퓨터를 사고 싶어해요.   Sophia also wants to buy a
                                  computer.

The past-tense form of ~고 싶어요 is not ~었/았고 싶어요 but ~고 싶었어요.

집에 일찍 가고 싶어요.   I want to go home early.
집에 일찍 가고 싶었어요.   I wanted to go home early.

Exercises

1. Ask your partner these questions.

(1)   저녁에 뭐 먹고 싶어요?
(2)   이번 주말에 뭐 하고 싶어요?
(3)   방학에 어디 가고 싶으세요?
(4)   생일에 무슨 선물을 받고 싶으세요?
(5)   무슨 차를 타고 싶으세요?

2. Change the following sentences as in the example.

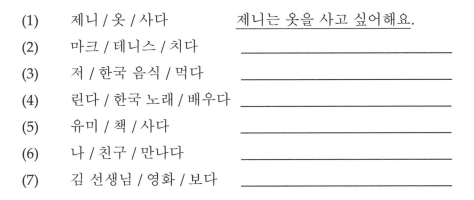

(1)   제니 / 옷 / 사다   제니는 옷을 사고 싶어해요.
(2)   마크 / 테니스 / 치다   _____
(3)   저 / 한국 음식 / 먹다   _____
(4)   린다 / 한국 노래 / 배우다 _____
(5)   유미 / 책 / 사다   _____
(6)   나 / 친구 / 만나다   _____
(7)   김 선생님 / 영화 / 보다   _____

| G10.3 | The sentence ending ~(으)ㄴ데요/는데요 |

Examples

(1) A: 여기가 김 교수님 연구실이지요?
     B: 네, 그런**데요**.
     A: 김 교수님 지금 계세요?
     B: 지금 안 계시**는데요**.   He is not here now.

(2) A: 날씨가 좋은데 밖에 놀러 가요.   The weather is nice;
                                                   let's go out to play.
     B: 미안해요. 약속이 있**는데요**.   I'm sorry. I have a
                                                   prior engagement.

Notes

1. The sentence ending ~(으)ㄴ데요/는데요 is an extended usage of the clausal connective ~(으)ㄴ데/는데 (G10.1). By using ~(으)ㄴ데요/는데요, the speaker presents background information and lets the listener figure out what to do. Thus, it may be used as an expression of politeness.

     For example, in (1) above speaker B uses 안 계시는데요 to respond instead of 안 계세요, so that speaker A can figure out what to do next. "Would you like to leave a message?" or "Can I do anything for you?" is implied.

Compare the use of ~어요/아요 and of ~(으)ㄴ데요/는데요 in the following telephone dialogue:

     A: 마크 씨 집에 있어요?   Is Mark home?

     B: a. 지금 없어요.   He is not at home.
                                            (direct/assertive)

         b. 지금 없는데요.   He is not at home. (Is there
                                            anything I can do for you?)
                                            (indirect)

2. The ~(으)ㄴ데요/는데요 form is also used to deal with delicate situations such as disagreement, denial, and rejection. For instance, speaker B in (2) above avoids a direct rejection by conveying his situation implicitly. The ~(으)ㄴ데요/는데요 form allows speakers to avoid explicitly stating their intentions.

Exercise

Respond to the following sentences using the ~(으)ㄴ데요/는데요 form to express disagreement, denial, or rejection.

(1)   시간 좀 있으세요?   지금은 시간 없는데요.

(2)   내일 파티에 같이 가요.   죽제가 많이 있는데요

(3)   박 교수님 지금 계세요?   지금 안 계시는데요

(4)   오늘 시험이 어땠어요?   괜잖는데요 ㅡ

(5)   이 식당 음식이 맛있지요?   _____

(6)   같이 공원에 놀러 가요.   _____

어ㅣ ㅁㅣ 아정 ?

Conversation 2   늦어서 죄송합니다.

(Mark is late for the Korean placement test.)

(똑똑)

교수님: 네, 들어오세요.

마크: 늦어서[G10.4] 죄송합니다.

          차가 많이 막혀서 늦었습니다.

교수님: 교통이 무척 복잡하지요? 뭐 타고 왔어요?

마크: 여기까지 직접 오는[G10.5] 버스가 없어서

          택시를 타고 왔어요.

교수님: 택시도 괜찮지만 다음부터는 지하철을 타세요.

          지하철이 빠르고 편해요.

마크: 여기 오는 지하철은 몇 호선이에요?

교수님: 2호선이에요.

NEW WORDS

NOUN		VERB	
가수	singer	늦다	to be late
교통	transportation; traffic	들어오다	to come in
날	day	이사하다	to move
머리	① head;	**ADJECTIVE**	
	② hair	막히다	to be blocked, congested
일	④ event		
ADVERB		복잡하다	to be crowded
다음부터(는)	from next time	불편하다	to be uncomfortable, inconvenient
무척	very much		
직접	directly	빠르다	to be fast
SUFFIX		아프다	to be sick
~어서/아서	clausal connective (cause)	편하다	to be comfortable, convenient
~는	noun modifying form	**CONJUNCTION**	
		그렇지만	but, however

NEW EXPRESSIONS

1. 죄송합니다 'I am very sorry' literally means 'I feel guilty'. This expression is appropriate in speaking to a person of higher status. 미안합니다 'I am sorry' (lit. I feel uncomfortable) is usually used to a peer.

2. 교통이 복잡하지요? 'Traffic is congested, isn't it?' literally means 'Traffic is complicated, isn't it?' 교통 alone means 'transportation', not 'traffic congestion'.

3. 똑똑 expresses a door knocking sound equivalent to "knock knock."

Exercises

1. Fill in the blanks with appropriate verbs or adjectives.

　(1)　서울에는 차가 아주 많아요. 그래서 교통이 _____.

　(2)　오늘 아침 9시 30분에 일어났어요. 그래서 10시 한국어 수업에 _____.

(3)   택시는 _____. 그렇지만 너무 비싸요.

(4)   보통 오후 6시에는 차가 많이 _____.

2. Ask your classmates the following questions.

(1)   동네/학교 근처 교통이 어때요?

(2)   학교에 어떻게 오세요?

(3)   왜 자전거/버스/지하철/차를 타고 오세요?

       (or 왜 걸어서 오세요?)

GRAMMAR

G10.4   The clausal connective ~어서/아서 (cause)

Examples

(1)	A:	왜 한국어를 배우세요?	Why do you study Korean?
	B:	**재미있어서** 배워요.	It's fun, and so I am learning it.
	C:	한국어를 잘 하고 **싶어서** 배워요.	I want to speak Korean well, and so I learn.
(2)	A:	오늘 아침 수업에 왜 늦었어요?	
	B:	일이 **있어서** 늦었어요.	

(3)   어제 머리가 **아파서** 타이레놀을 먹었어요.

(4)   집 근처에 마켓이 **없어서** 불편해요.

Some fixed uses of ~어서/아서:

(5)   **늦어서** 죄송합니다.   I'm sorry for being late.

(6)   전화 **주셔서** 감사합니다/고맙습니다.   Thank you very much for giving me a call.

Notes

1. The pattern [Clause 1~어서/아서 + clause 2] is used to give a cause or reason for the event described in clause 2. Because [Clause 1~어서/아서] expresses a reason or a cause, it is often used in response to the question 왜 'Why', as in examples (1) and (2).

2. Note that there is a close temporal relation between the two events in example (3). That is, the event in clause 2 (taking some Tylenol) cannot take place before the event in clause 1 (having a headache).

3. The choice between ~어서 and ~아서 is determined by the same principle that determines the choice between ~어요 and ~아요 as in the table provided below.

Dictionary form	~어요/아요	~어서/아서
좋다	좋아요	좋아서
아프다	아파요	아파서
늦다	늦어요	늦어서
재미있다	재미있어요	재미있어서
복잡하다	복잡해요	복잡해서
가깝다	가까워요	가까워서

4. In example (3), ~어서/아서 in the first clause never takes a tense marker. For example, unlike English, the past-tense suffix cannot occur in 머리가 아파서 (Clause 1) even though the tense of the main clause (Clause 2) is past, as in 타이레놀을 먹었어요.

5. The main clause (Clause 2) may be omitted if the context makes clear to the listener what is omitted. The polite ending ~요 should be attached to maintain the polite speech level.

A: 왜 한국어를 배우세요? Why are you studying Korean?
B: 한국에 가고 **싶어서**요. Because I want to go to Korea.

Exercises

1. Practice as in the example.

(1)   오후에 수업이 없다 / 테니스를 치다

오후에 수업이 **없어서** 테니스를 쳐요.

(2)   날씨가 덥다 / 수영하다

날씨가 더워서 수영해요

(3)   교통이 복잡하다 / 지하철로 학교에 가다

교통이 복잡해서 지하철로 학교에 가요

(4)   한국어를 배우고 싶다 / 서울에 가다

한국어를 배우고 싶어서 서울에 가요

(5)   집에서 마켓까지 가깝다 / 걸어서 가다

집에서 마켓까지 가까워서 걸어서 가요

(6)   날씨가 춥다/ 그냥 집에 있다

날씨가 추워서 그냥 집에 있어요

2. Answer the following questions using ~어서/아서.

(1)   왜 이 수업을 들어요?   한국어 배우고 싶어서

(2)   오늘 왜 수업에 늦었어요?   차가 없다 ... 없어서

(3)   어제 왜 학교에 안 왔어요?   몸이 안 좋아서

G10.5   The noun-modifying form [Verb~는] + N

Examples

(1)   한국어를 **배우는** 학생들이 많아요.   There are many students
who study Korean.

(2)   수업 **없는** 날은 뭐하세요?

(3)   기숙사에 **사는** 사람이 누구예요?   Who is the person who lives in the dormitory?

(4)   A: 테니스 잘 **치는** 사람을 아세요?   Do you know a person who plays tennis well?

B: 제 친구**인** 스티브가 잘 쳐요.   Steve, who is my friend, does well.

(5)   제가 보고 **싶은** 영화는 '괴물'이에요.   *The Host* is the movie that I want to watch.

Notes

1. A construction consisting of [Verb/Adjective~는/(으)ㄴ] + N is called a relative clause. It is a type of noun-modifying construction. Compare the word order of a noun-modifying construction in English and Korean.

English: The newspaper that I read is the *Times*.
             a   b   c

Korean: 내가 읽**는**   신문은   타임스예요.
             b   a   c

As shown above, relative clauses in Korean have the following characteristics:

a.   In Korean, the modifying clause 내가 읽는 'that I read' precedes the modified noun 신문 'the newspaper', whereas in English the modifying clause "that I read" follows the modified noun "the newspaper."

b.   In Korean, there are no relative pronouns such as "which," "who," and "that" as in English.

c.   The topic marker 은/는 cannot occur in a relative clause. 이/가 is used instead: 내가 읽는 책 'the book that I read', not 나는 읽는 책.

2. For /르/ irregular verbs, the stem-final /르/ is deleted before ~는 or ~시.

Dictionary form	~는 form	~(으)시는 honorific form
살다 to live	사는	사시는
만들다 to make	만드는	만드시는
알다 to know	아는	아시는

기숙사에 사는 학생   a student who lives in the dorm
음식을 만드시는 어머니   a mother who makes food
잘 아는 사이   a relationship that is close

Note that the adjectives 멀다 and 길다 become 먼 and 긴.

3. 있다/없다 (e.g., 맛있다/ 맛없다) occurs with ~는 like any other verbs when the relative clause is in the present tense (G9.2).

책상 위에 있는 게 뭐예요?   What is that thing that is on the
                            desk?

수업이 없는 날 뭐 하세요?   What do you do on the days that
                            you don't have classes?

4. The copula ~(이)다/아니다 becomes ~인/아닌 or ~이신/아니신 for noun-modifying forms.

고등학생인 내 동생은   My younger sibling, who is a
지금 도서관에서 공부해요.   high school student, is studying at
                            the library now.

의사이신 우리 아버지를 만나세요. Meet my father, who is a medical
                            doctor.

학생 아닌 사람은 수업을 못 들어요. Those who are not students cannot
                            take classes.

5. As noted in G9.2, adjectives take the (으)ㄴ form as in 큰 (크다), 예쁜 (예쁘다), 먼 (멀다) and the desirative auxiliary verb ~고 싶다 takes the (으)ㄴ form as in ~고 싶은.

저는 키('height')가 커요. 그렇지만 키가 작은 사람을 좋아해요.
제가 먹고 싶은 음식은 햄버거예요.

Exercises

1. Draw a square around the noun-modifying phrase, and circle the modified noun in each sentence. Then, translate the sentence into English.

(1)　신문을 읽으시는 분은 우리 어머니세요.
　　　The person who is reading the newspaper is my mother.

(2)　여기가 제가 사는 동네예요.
　　　That~~Over there~~ is the neighborhood I live in

(3)　이건 마이클이 자주 듣는 노래예요.
　　　That This is the song Michael listens to often.

(4)　방에 계시는 분은 우리 할머니세요.　aw?
　　　The person in the room is my grandmother

(5)　저는 김 선생님이 가르치시는 수업을 들어요.
　　　I take the class Professor Kim teaches.

(6)　민지가 이사하는 집이 여기서 멀어요?　far from here?
　　　Is the house minji is moving to close?

2. Describe the following nouns, using the construction [Verb~는] + N.

(1)　가수　　　　가수는 노래를 하는 사람이에요.

(2)　학생　　　　_____

(3)　룸메이트　　_____

(4)　선생님　　　_____

Narration 호주 학생 '마크'

마크

저는 호주 사람입니다. 한국어와 한국 문화를 배우고
싶어서 지난 달에 서울에 왔습니다. 호주에서 일 년 동안
한국어를 배웠습니다. 호주에는 한국어를 가르치는
학교가 많이 있습니다. 저는 이번 학기에 서울대학교
대학원에서 한국 문화를 전공합니다. 그리고 박 교수님이
가르치시는 한국어 수업도 듣습니다. 지난 달에 박 교수님
연구실에서 한국어 시험을 봤습니다. 그런데 차가 많이
막혀서 10분 늦었습니다. 서울은 교통이 무척 복잡하고
사람들이 굉장히 많습니다. 그렇지만 재미있는 일들도
많이 있습니다. 교통이 불편해서 저는 다음 주에 학교
기숙사로 이사합니다.

Exercises

1. Read the narration and answer the following questions.

    (1)   마크는 어디에서 왔습니까? *1 마크는 호로주에서 왔습니다*

    (2)   왜 서울에 왔습니까? *2 한국어 와 한국문화를 배우고 싶어서*

    (3)   마크는 어디에서 무슨 공부를 합니까? *3 마크는 서울 대학교에서 한국문화를 공부합니다.*

    (4)   마크는 무슨 시험을 봤습니까? 왜 봤습니까?

    (5)   마크는 왜 시험에 늦었습니까?

    (6)   서울의 교통은 어떻습니까?

    (7)   마크는 언제, 왜 기숙사로 이사합니까?

2. Retell the story in the narration to your partner using your own words.

3. Now, summarize the narration in your own words using 5-6 sentences.

4.) 한국말 시험과2봤습니다. 10분 늦었서 & 연구 실에 한국어 시험을 봤습니다.

5.) 차가 안늦이 막혔어요

CULTURE

6.) 무척 복잡해요.

7.) 교통이 불편해서요.

서울의 대중 교통 (Public transportation in Seoul)

Like many other big cities worldwide, Seoul has a well-connected public transportation network that is affordable, efficient, safe, and clean. Even though you don't own a car, you can get around the city and its vicinity without major inconvenience. The main means of ground transportation are bus, subway, and taxi. Recently, public transportation became easier and faster to use with the introduction of 교통카드, an electronic transportation pass. Now you can pay for the bus, subway, and taxi by simply tapping your pass on a receiver.

1. 버스 (Bus)

There are four different types of buses in the metropolitan area:

- 시내버스: The most common type of bus. They go from one district of the city to another.
- 좌석버스: Express bus with more comfortable seats. They usually run longer routes than 시내버스 and are faster with fewer stops.
- 마을버스: Small-sized local bus. They usually run shorter and more complicated routes within a local area.
- 고속버스: Long-distance express bus. They run inter-city and inter-state routes all around the country. Oftentimes, you have to go to a bus terminal to take them.

2. 지하철 (Subway)

The subway is probably the most convenient means of public transportation in Seoul. Seoul's subway network is one of the world's longest with nine central lines in the city area and five additional lines stretching over the boundary of the capital. Line 2, the busiest line, carries more than two million passengers a day, accounting for nearly 40 percent of the population using the subway.

3. 택시 (Taxi)

Not like the yellow cabs in New York City or the black cabs in London, the taxis in Seoul come in various colors and types. One exception is 모범택시, a bigger and more luxurious kind of taxi with better service. They are all black with a yellow sign on the top.

USAGE

A. Visiting a professor's office: How to start a conversation

When you enter a professor's office, you can introduce yourself and state the reason for your visit as shown in the following dialogue:

마크: 저어, 여기가 김 교수님 연구실이지요?
김 교수님: 네, 그런데요. 어떻게 오셨어요?
마크: 저는 마크 스미스입니다. 이번 학기에
            한국어 수업을 듣고 싶습니다.

To ask the purpose of a visit, one says 어떻게 오셨어요? 'How can I help you?' (lit. How did you come?). Another way of asking is 무슨 일로 오셨어요? (lit. For what business did you come?).

[Exercise] Role-play: start a conversation in the following context: A student visits a professor to take a placement test before taking a Korean class.

B. Giving one's biographical information

자기 소개 'self-introduction' may include the following information, among other things.

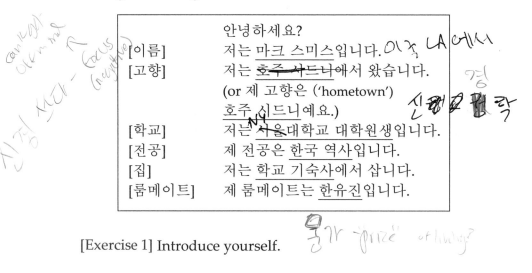

	안녕하세요?
[이름]	저는 마크 스미스입니다.
[고향]	저는 호주 시드니에서 왔습니다.
	(or 제 고향은 ('hometown')
	호주 시드니예요.)
[학교]	저는 서울대학교 대학원생입니다.
[전공]	제 전공은 한국 역사입니다.
[집]	저는 학교 기숙사에서 삽니다.
[룸메이트]	제 룸메이트는 한유진입니다.

[Exercise 1] Introduce yourself.

[Exercise 2] Interview a classmate and obtain the type of information given in the dialogue above. Then, introduce your classmate to the rest of the class based on what you have found out from the interview.

C. Expressing reservations

The connective form ~(으)ㄴ데/는데 is used to give background information for another situation. In conversation this pattern is also used to express reservations about someone or something, as illustrated below.

A: 기숙사가 어때요?
B: 학교에서 가까워서 좋은데 방이 좀 작아요.
A: 룸메이트는 어때요?
B: 착하고 좋은데 밤 늦게까지('until late at night') 음악을
      자주 들어요.
A: 기숙사 음식은 어때요?
B: 다 괜찮은데 김치(kimchi)가 없어요.

[Exercise] Make up dialogues on the following topics, using ~(으)ㄴ데/는데 whenever possible.

(1)　　한국어 수업

(2)　　요즘 날씨

(3)　　(your school) 캠퍼스

(4)　　학교 식당 음식

D. Making an apology and giving reasons

When you apologize for being late for an appointment, use 늦어서 미안합니다 (or 늦어서 죄송합니다) 'I'm sorry for being late'. When you want to explain in detail your reason for being late, use the following pattern:

reason/cause: ~어서/아서 늦었습니다.

A:　　오늘 왜 한국어 수업에 늦었어요?

B:　　a.　　차가 많이 막혀서 늦었어요.
　　　　　　　Because traffic was congested.

　　　　b.　　차 사고가 나서 늦었어요.
　　　　　　　Because I had a car accident.

　　　　c.　　차가 고장이 나서 늦었어요.
　　　　　　　Because my car broke down.

　　　　d.　　늦잠을 자서 늦었어요.
　　　　　　　Because I overslept.

[Exercise] Role-play: using the question word '왜' and the clausal connective ~어서/아서, ask questions and provide reasons.

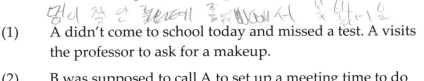

(1)　　A didn't come to school today and missed a test. A visits the professor to ask for a makeup.

(2)　　B was supposed to call A to set up a meeting time to do their assignment together, but B didn't.

(3)　　B invited A to his/her birthday party but A didn't show up.

Lesson 10 - At a Professor's Office

CONVERSATION 1: I don't have time today.
(Mark introduces himself to Professor Park and makes an arrangement to take the Korean placement test.)

Mark:	Nice to meet you, sir.
Professor:	Hello. How can I help you?
Mark:	My name is Mark Smith. I major in Korean cultures and I would like to take a Korean language course this semester.
Professor:	I see. How long have you been studying Korean?
Mark:	I studied Korean for a year at the University of Sydney.
Professor:	Then you should take the Korean placement test this afternoon.
Mark:	I'm sorry but I don't have time today.
Professor:	Then come tomorrow morning at nine o'clock to take the test.
Mark:	That works. Then I'll see you tomorrow.

CONVERSATION 2: I'm sorry for being late.
(Mark is late for the Korean placement test.)

	(knock knock)
Professor:	Come in.
Mark:	I'm sorry for being late. I was stuck in heavy traffic.
Professor:	The traffic is pretty bad, isn't it? How did you get here?
Mark:	The buses don't come here directly so I took a taxi.
Professor:	Taxi is fine but take the subway next time. It is fast and convenient.
Mark:	Which subway line gets me here?
Professor:	Line 2.

NARRATION: Australian student Mark

I'm Australian. I came to Seoul a month ago because I wanted to learn its language and culture. I studied Korean for a year in Australia. In Australia, there are many schools with a Korean language program. I study Korean cultures this semester at a graduate school at Seoul University. I'm also taking the Korean language course given by Professor Park. I went to Professor Park's office last month to take the placement test. But I ended up being ten minutes late because of heavy traffic. The traffic in Seoul is overwhelming, and the streets are crowded with people. However, there are lots of things to entertain you, too. Since the transportation is inconvenient, I'm moving into the school dormitory next week.

11과 기숙사 생활 [Living in a Dormitory]

Conversation 1 | 차 한 잔 하실래요?

(Woojin and Minji meet at the school cafeteria.)

우진: 어, 민지 씨 아니세요? 뭐 하세요?

민지: 차 마시고 있어요.^{G11.1}

      우진 씨도 차 한 잔 하실래요?^{G11.2}

우진: 네, 저도 마시고 싶었는데 잘 됐네요.

민지: 한국 생활이 어때요?

우진: 참 재미있어요. 친구도 많이 사귀었어요.

      그리고 기숙사 생활도 편하고 재미있어요.

민지: 우진 씨는 방을 혼자 쓰세요?

우진: 아니요, 룸메이트가 있어요.

민지: 어떤 사람이에요?

우진: 호주에서 왔는데 한국을 정말 좋아하고
      한국말도 잘 해요. 그리고 아주 친절하고
      착해요.

"웃긴- funny (adj.)
한 세다
춘방"-inthe middle
11과 기숙사 생활   53

NEW WORDS

NOUN		VERB	
갈비	*kalbi* (barbecued spareribs)	되다	to become, get, turn into
물	water	눈(이) 오다	to snow
바닷가	beach	만들다	to make
밴쿠버	Vancouver	사귀다	to make friends
불고기	*pulgogi* (roast meat)	쓰다	② to use
생활	daily life, living	**ADJECTIVE**	
어젯밤	last night	착하다	to be good-natured, kind-hearted
차	tea		
청바지	blue jeans	친절하다	to be kind, considerate
캐나다	Canada	**SUFFIX**	
COUNTER		~(으)ㄹ래요	Would you like to . . .?/ I would like to . . .
잔	glass, cup		(intention)
PRE-NOUN			
어떤	which, what kind of	~고 있다	am/are/is ~ing

NEW EXPRESSIONS

1. 어, 민지 씨 아니세요? 'Oh, aren't you Minji?' expresses Yujin's surprise at meeting Minji unexpectedly.

2. 잘 됐네요 is an idiomatic expression, meaning 'It sounds good' (lit. It has turned out well). The dictionary form of 됐네요 is 되다 'to become, get, turn into'.

The verb 되다 has many functions, as shown below.

   a.   to become
       남동생은 내년에 대학생이 됩니다.   My younger brother will become a college student next year.

   b.   to work out, turn out
       참 잘 됐네요.   That's great (lit. It worked out well).

c.   idiomatic expressions:

. . . 어떻게 됩니까/돼요?	What is/are . . .?
주소가 어떻게 됩니까?	What is your address?
나이가 어떻게 되세요?	What is your age?
부모님 성함이 어떻게 되십니까?	What are your parents' names?

3. 사귀었어요 is often pronounced [사겨써요], although it is never written that way.

4. 어떤 is a noun-modifying form of 어떻다 'to be how' and denotes an unspecified person or thing. 어떤 occurs both as an interrogative meaning 'what kind (type) of?' and as an indefinite, 'certain, some'.

Exercises

1. Connect each of the phrases from the left column with a predicate on the right.

여자 친구를	•	•	많아요
차를	•	•	되고 싶어요
잔에 물이	•	•	사귀었어요
의사가	•	•	마셔요

2. Answer the following questions:

(1)   어떤 일을 하고 싶어요?

(2)   어떤 친구를 사귀고 싶어요?

(3)   어떤 음악을 듣고 싶어요?

(4)   어떤 생일 선물을 받고 싶어요?

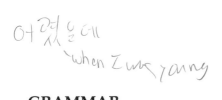

어렸을때
　　when I was young

GRAMMAR

G11.1 The progressive form ~고 있다

Examples

(1)　남동생은 친구하고 불고기를 만들**고 있어요**.

(2)　A:　지금 뭐 하**고 있어요**?　　　What are you doing now?

　　　B:　음악 듣**고 있는데요**.　　　I'm listening to music.

(3)　지금 밖에 눈이 **오고 있어요**.

(4)　아버지는 신문을 읽**고 계세요**.　　My father is reading the
　　　　　　　　　　　　　　　　　　newspaper.

Notes

1. ~고 있다 expresses the continuation or progression of an action. Only verbs (not adjectives) can occur in this construction.

2. Various forms of ~고 있다:

	Default forms	Plain	Subject honorific
Non-past	~고 있다	~고 있어요	~고 계세요
Past	~고 있었다	~고 있었어요	~고 계셨어요

　동생은 방에서 놀고 있어요
　저는 어젯밤 9시에 친구하고 전화하고 있었어요.
　어머니는 지금 영화를 보고 계세요.
　아침에 아버지는 신문을 보고 계셨어요.

Exercises

1. Change the verbs into the progressive form ~고 있다 or ~고 계시다.

(1)   동생이 방에서 (자다)   <u>자고 있어요</u>.

(2)   저는 지금 도서관에서 (일하다)   _____

(3)   부모님께서 캐나다 밴쿠버에서 (살다) _____

(4)   소피아는 교실에서 (공부하다)   _____

(5)   마크는 마이클하고 책을 같이 (쓰다) _____

2. Practice with your partner as in the example.

(1)   A: 동수는 지금 뭐 하고 있어요?
       B: 자전거를 타고 있어요.

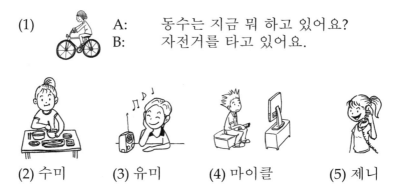

(2) 수미   (3) 유미   (4) 마이클   (5) 제니

3. Practice the above dialogues one more time using the past-tense form ~고 있었어요 as in the example.

A: 동수는 어제 아침에 뭐 하고 있었어요?
B: 자전거를 타고 있었어요.

4. Describe each person's activity, using the construction [~고 있는] + N (see G10.5), and ask your partner who each one of them is.

(1)   A: 자전거를 타고 있는 사람은 누구예요?
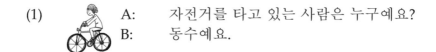
       B: 동수예요.

(2) 린다   (3) 수잔   (4) 마이클   (5) 팀

(6) 스티브   (7) 수미   (8) 폴   (9) 마이클 & 유미

G11.2 Intentional ~(으)ㄹ래요

Examples

(1)	A:	뭐 **먹을래요**?	What would you like to eat?
	B:	저는 갈비 **먹을래요**.	I'd like to eat *kalbi*.
	C:	저는 불고기 **먹을래요**.	I'd like to eat *pulgogi*.

(2)	A:	이번 주말에 영화 보러 **갈래요**?	
	B:	네, 좋아요. 같이 가요.	

(3)	A:	물 좀 **주실래요**?	Would you give me some water?
	B:	네, 여기 있어요.	

Notes

1. ~(으)ㄹ래요 is used to ask the intention of the listener in questions and refers to the speaker's intention in statements.

2. ~(으)ㄹ래요? in questions is used in less formal settings. A more formal and polite form is ~(으)시겠어요?

3. The formation of ~(으)ㄹ래요 with verbs in /ㄷ/ and /ㄹ/ is demonstrated below.

Dictionary form	~어요/아요	~(으)ㄹ래요
걷다 to walk	걸어요	걸을래요
만들다 to make	만들어요	만들래요

Exercises

1. Change the verbs in the box below with different suffixes.

	오다	먹다	타다	듣다
~어요/아요	와요	먹어요	타요	들어요
~(으)ㄹ래요	올래요	먹을래요	탈래요	들을래요
~습/ㅂ니다	옵니다	먹습니다	탑니다	들습니다

2. Practice as in the example.

(1)   뭐 마실 거예요?   (커피) 커피 마실래요.

(2)   무슨 영화 볼 거예요?   (액션 영화) 액션영화를 볼래요

(3)   무슨 옷을 살 거예요?   (청바지) 청바지 살래요

(4)   주말에 어디 갈 거예요?   (바닷가) 바닷가 갈래요

(5)   뭐 먹을 거예요?   (불고기) 불고기 먹을래요

(6)   내일 저녁에 뭐 할 거예요? 밥 먹을래요

식당을 갈래요

Conversation 2   연극 보러 갈까요?

(Minji and Woojin chat in the dormitory lounge.)

우진: 시간이 참 빠르지요? 벌써 한 학기가 다
　　　　끝났어요. 이번 학기에 몇 과목 들었어요?

민지: 다섯 과목 들었어요.

우진: 다섯 과목이나[G11.3] 들었어요?
　　　　저는 세 과목밖에[G11.3] 안 들었어요.

민지: 월요일부터 금요일까지 매일 수업이 있어서
　　　　너무 바빴어요. 우진 씨는 이번 학기 잘
　　　　보냈어요?

우진: 숙제가 많아서 저도 좀 바빴어요.
　　　　다음 주부터는 좀 쉬고 싶어요.

민지: 그럼 시험 끝나고 같이
　　　　연극 보러 갈까요?[G11.4]

우진: 네, 좋아요. 보고 싶은
　　　　연극 있어요?

민지: 글쎄요. 인터넷으로
　　　　같이 알아볼까요?

우진: 네, 그래요.

NEW WORDS

NOUN		ADJECTIVE	
골프	golf	힘(이) 들다	to be hard
기차	train	**ADVERB**	
연극	play	다	all
인터넷	Internet	벌써	already
입구	entrance	**PARTICLE**	
VERB		까지	to/until/through (time)
끝나다	to be over, finished	밖에	nothing but, only
쉬다	to rest	부터	from (time) . . .
알아보다	to find out, check out	(이)나	as much/many as
		SUFFIX	
찾다	to find, look for	~(으)ㄹ까요?	Shall I/we . . .?; Do you
춤(을) 추다	to dance		think that . . .?
		글쎄요	Well; It's hard to say

NEW EXPRESSIONS

1. The pattern [time]부터 [time]까지 'from . . . to . . .' is usually used for temporal expressions. [place]에서 [place]까지, though also translated 'from . . . to . . .', is used for location (Lesson 6, Conv. 1).

> 부터: a starting point in time or location 'from'
> 까지: an ending point in time or location '(all the way) to, until, through'

> Time: . . . 부터 . . . 까지
> 한국어 수업은 9시부터 10시까지 있어요.
> 아침부터 저녁까지 일해요.

> Location: . . . 에서 . . . 까지
> 서울에서 뉴욕까지 비행기로 얼마나 걸려요?
> 기숙사에서 교실까지 걸어서 얼마나 걸려요?

2. 글쎄요 'Well (I am not quite sure)' is used when one is not quite ready to give an answer. It can also be used to show hesitation or to express a refusal in a polite and indirect way.

> A: 이번 주에 같이 영화 보러 갈래요?
> B: 글쎄요. 다음 주에 시험이 있는데요.

전 - before *후 - after*

2년 전부터

6 개월

Exercise

Answer the following questions using 부터/까지.

(1) 몇 시부터 몇 시까지 자요?

(2) 오늘 수업이 언제 있어요?

(3) 언제부터 한국어를 배웠어요?

(4) 언제부터 [뉴욕, 보스톤, 로스앤젤레스, . . .]에서 살았어요?

(5) 한국어 수업은 몇 시부터 몇 시까지 있어요?

GRAMMAR

밖에 -> always negative

G11.3	N(이)나 vs. N밖에

Examples

(1) A: 이번 학기에 몇 과목 들었어요? How many classes did you take this semester?

  B: 다섯 과목 들었어요. I took five classes.

  A: 다섯 과목**이나** 들었어요? You took five [that many]?

  저는 세 과목**밖에** 안 들었는데요. I took only three.

(2) A: 집에서 학교까지 얼마나 걸려요? How long does it take from your home to school?

  B: 걸어서 5분**밖에** 안 걸려요. It takes only five minutes on foot.

  A: 아, 그래요?

  저는 차로 한 시간**이나** 걸려요.

(3) 남자 시계를 찾는데 여자 시계**밖에** 없어요.

Notes

1. When attached to an expression of quantity, the particle (이)나 indicates that the quantity in question is more than the speaker's expectation. It shows surprise or shock at the large quantity. (이)나 can often be translated 'as much/many as', but it also implies 'that many/much' along with an expression of quantity, as in (1). 이나 is used when the expression ends in a consonant, 나 when the expression ends in a vowel.

파티에 스무 명이나 왔어요. vs. 내일 시험이 다섯 개나 있어요.

2. [N 밖에 + negative] 'nothing/nobody/no . . . but N; only N' is used when the speaker feels that the amount of the item mentioned is smaller than the speaker's expectation. Compare the answers in (a) and (b) below.

A: 교실에서 기숙사 입구까지 얼마나 걸려요?

B: (a) 걸어서 5분 걸려요.   It takes five minutes
                                                on foot. (neutral
                                                description)

      (b) 걸어서 5분밖에 안 걸려요.   It takes only five
                                                minutes on foot.
                                                (less than expected)

More examples are given below.

A: 파티에 누가 왔어요?
B: 마크밖에 안 왔어요.

A: 어제 몇 시간 잤어요?
B: 세 시간밖에 못 잤어요.

3. [N밖에 + negative] is not used in commands; 만 'only' is used instead.

한국어로만 말하세요.
경제학 숙제만 하세요.

Exercises

1. Using (이)나 or 밖에, indicate your surprise at the quantity.

(1) A: 파티에 사람들 많이 왔어요?

  B: 네, 여덟 명 왔어요.

  A: <u>여덟 명 밖에 안 왔어요?</u>

(2) A: 이번 학기에 몇 과목 들으세요?

  B: 여섯 과목 들어요.

  A: <u>여섯 과목이나 들어요</u>

한 → (for items)
People

(3) A: 어제 잘 잤어요?

쯤 – approx ~
(numbers)
(time)

  B: 4시간쯤 잤어요.

  A: <u>4시간 밖에 안 잤어요?</u>

(4) A: 한국어 숙제 했어요?

이나

  B: 네, 그런데 <u>5시간 밖에 안 걸렸어요</u>

  A: 저도 5시간 걸렸어요.

(5) A: 스타워즈 (Star Wars) 영화 봤어요?

  B: 네, 너무 재미있어서 <u>세 번 밖이나 봤어요</u>

  A: 그래요? 저도 세 번 봤어요.

2. Answer the following questions, using (이)나 or 밖에.

(1) A: 어제 많이 잤어요?   [7시간]

  B: a. 일곱 시간밖에 못 잤어요.

    b. 일곱 시간이나 잤어요.

(2) 돈이 얼마 있어요?   [100불]

(3) 집에 책이 많이 있어요?   [40권]

(4) 교실에 의자가 몇 개 있어요?   [6개]

(5)   지난 주에 시험 있었어요?   [4개]

(6)   한국어 수업에 학생이 많아요?   [20명]

(7)   어제 파티에 사람들이 많이 왔어요? [12명]

G11.4   Asking someone's opinion: ~(으)ㄹ까요?

Examples

(1)   한국어로 말**할까요**?   Shall I/we speak in Korean?

(2)   내일 날씨가 좋**을까요**?   Do you think tomorrow's
                                        weather will be good?

(3)   기차로 갈까요, 버스로 **갈까요**?   Shall I/we go by train or by
                                        bus?

(4)   같이 춤추러 **갈까요**?   Shall we go dancing?

Notes

1. The basic function of ~(으)ㄹ까요? is to ask for the listener's opinion.
When the speaker is (a part of) the subject, ~(으)ㄹ까요 often connotes a
suggestion or an offer ("shall I/we?") in addition to asking the listener's
opinion. This structure is strictly a question. It cannot be used to mean "I
shall do."

뭘 먹을까요?	What shall we eat?
갈비 먹을까요?	Shall we eat *kalbi*? / How about eating *kalbi*?
커피 마실까요?	Shall we drink some coffee?
제가 갈까요?	Shall I go? (= May I suggest that I go?)

2. When the subject is a third person, ~(으)ㄹ까요? 'Do you think that . . .?'
is used to seek the listener's opinion.

| 시험이 어려울까요? | Do you think that the exam will be difficult? |
| 제니가 파티에 올까요? | Do you think that Jenny will come to the party? |

3. The pattern ~(으)ㄹ까요? is also used for questions that offer a choice of alternatives, as in 영어로 말할까요, 한국어로 말할까요? 'Shall I/we speak in English or shall I/we speak in Korean?' Notice that in Korean the whole predicate is repeated, whereas in English the predicate does not repeat often (e.g, Shall I/we speak in English or in Korean?).

4. The form ~(으)ㄹ까요? has the following variations:

    a. ~을까요? occurs after a verb or adjective stem ending in a consonant other than /ㄹ/.

    b. ~ㄹ까요? occurs after a verb or adjective stem ending in a vowel.

    c. ~까요? occurs after a verb or adjective stem ending in /ㄹ/.

	Dictionary form		~(으)ㄹ까요?
Stems ending in a consonant	먹다	to eat	먹을까요
	앉다	to sit down	앉을까요
	좋다	to be good	좋을까요
Stems ending in a vowel	만나다	to meet	만날까요
	말하다	to speak	말할까요
	크다	to be big	클까요
Stems with /ㄹ/	살다	to live	살까요
	멀다	to be far	멀까요
Stems with /ㅂ/	가깝다	to be near	가까울까요

When irregular predicates in /ㅂ/ occur with the ~(으)ㄹ까요? form, /ㅂ/ is changed to 우, as shown below.

가깝다	to be near	가까울까요
어렵다	to be difficult	어려울까요
쉽다	to be easy	쉬울까요

(Exceptions: 좁다 → 좁을까요, 넓다 → 넓을까요)

Exercises

1. Translate the following sentences into Korean.

(1)   Shall I call Lisa?

_____

(2)   Shall we play tennis together this weekend?

_____

(3)   What time shall I come tomorrow morning?

_____

(4)   Will the test be easy or difficult?

_____

(5)   Do you think that Sophia will come to the party?

_____

2. Make alternative sentences using ~(으)ㄹ까요? as in the example.

(1)   한국어 / 영어, 말하다

A: 한국어로 말할까요, 영어로 말할까요?

B: 한국어로 말하세요.

(2)   택시 / 버스, 타다

A: _____

B: _____

(3) 커피 / 차, 마시다

    A: _____

    B: _____

(4) 한국어 / 일본어, 연습하다

    A: _____

    B: _____

(5) 테니스 / 골프, 치다

    A: _____

    B: _____

Narration 캐나다 학생 '민지'

저는 서울에서 한국어를 배우고 있는 캐나다 학생입니다. 밴쿠버에서 왔고 나이는 스물두 살입니다. 지금 학교 기숙사에서 삽니다. 제 방 번호는 317호[1]이고 입구에서 두 번째[2] 방입니다. 지난 학기 동안 저는 벌써 여러 친구들을 사귀었습니다. 3층에 사는 우진 씨는 재미교포[3] 학생입니다. 우진 씨는 운동도 잘하고, 공부도 열심히 하고, 아주 친절합니다. 우진 씨는 호주 학생인 마크하고 방을 같이 씁니다. 마크 씨도 아주 친절하고 착한 친구입니다. 저는 우진 씨하고 마크 씨하고 기숙사 식당에서 자주 저녁을 먹습니다. 다음 주에 시험이 모두 끝납니다. 그래서 시험 끝나고 같이 연극을 보러 갈 겁니다.

1. 호: a room number (counter)
2. 두 번째: the second
3. 재미교포: a Korean American

Exercise

Read the narration and answer the following questions.

(1)   민지는 한국에서 무엇을 하고 있습니까?

(2)   민지는 기숙사 몇 호에서 살고 있습니까?

(3)   우진이는 어디에서 왔고, 어떤 학생입니까?

(4)   우진의 룸메이트는 누구입니까?

(5)   민지는 누구하고 자주 저녁을 먹습니까?

(6)   다음 주에는 무슨 일이 있습니까?

CULTURE

한국의 음악 (Music in Korea)

At the center of 한류, the surge of popularity for Korean pop culture, are Korean popular songs. Widely known as K-pop, Korean popular songs have generated interest in Korea and its culture all around the world. There have been some precedents to the K-pop singers who directed the attention of the world to the musical talent of Koreans. 장영주 (Sarah Chang), a genius Korean American violinist, surprised the world with her musical talent from the age of eight. 장한나 (Han-Na Chang) is a world-

class cellist who studied under a famous cello maestro. 조수미 (Sumi Jo) captivated the hearts of the world with her heavenly soprano, and 정명훈 (Myung-Whun Chung) ended a splendid career as an orchestra conductor in the field of Western classical music.

In the field of traditional Korean music, 김덕수 (Duk-Soo Kim) left an outstanding legacy. He modified traditional 풍물놀이 into 사물놀이. As opposed to the larger-scale, activity-oriented 풍물놀이, the new breed of traditional Korean music was a sophisticated quartet performance. The advent of 사물놀이 triggered the introduction of traditional Korean music to the world and helped many inspired musicians venture into the new area of traditional Korean music.

USAGE

A. Meeting someone by chance

When you run into someone you know, you can greet the person by saying any of the following:

민정 씨 아니세요?	Isn't this Minjung?
선생님, 안녕하세요?	Hello, professor.
스티브 씨, 뭐 하세요?	Hi, Steve. What you are doing?
오래간만이에요.	Long time no see.
반가워요.	(I'm) happy to see you.
어디 가세요?	Where are you going? (You do not necessarily expect an answer to this question.)
여기 웬 일이세요?	What brought you here?

[Exercise] Suppose you came across the following people in the following places. How would you start a conversation? Make up a dialogue, using the models shown above.

(1)   Meet a teacher on campus.

(2)   Meet a classmate in front of the dormitory elevator.

(3)   Meet a friend on the street whom you haven't seen for a long time.

(4)   Meet an acquaintance at the post office.

B. Extending, accepting, and declining invitations

When you are inviting someone over or asking about going out with someone, you normally start out by asking if the person has time.

A: 이번 주말에 시간 있어요?
B: 네, 괜찮아요.
A: 그럼, 춤추러 클럽 ('club')에 갈래요?
B: 네, 좋아요. 같이 가요.

[Exercise 1] Adapt the preceding dialogue to the pictures below.

(1)   (2)   (3)

When you are accepting an invitation, simply say 네. In declining an invitation, the sentence ending ~(으)ㄴ데요/는데요 is often used to soften the refusal (see G10.3).

A: 이번 주말에 영화 보러 갈래요?
B: 글쎄요. 좀 바쁜데요.
A: 그럼 다음 주말에는 어때요?
B: 미안해요. 다음 주말에는 벌써 약속이 있는데요.

The following pattern is commonly used when making suggestions.

[purpose](으)러 [place]에 _____~(으)ㄹ래요?

[Exercise 2] Practice the following dialogue based on the pictures.

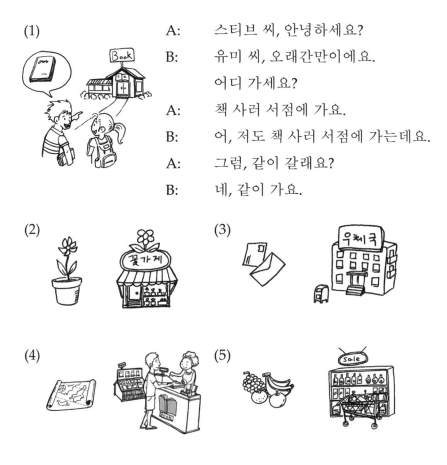

(1) A: 스티브 씨, 안녕하세요?

B: 유미 씨, 오래간만이에요.

어디 가세요?

A: 책 사러 서점에 가요.

B: 어, 저도 책 사러 서점에 가는데요.

A: 그럼, 같이 갈래요?

B: 네, 같이 가요.

(2)

(3)

(4)

(5)

C. Setting up a get-together

Example

민지: 우진 씨, 오늘 날씨도 좋은데
  테니스 같이 안 칠래요?

우진: 그래요. 그럼 오늘 칠까요?

민지: 몇 시에 시간 있으세요?

우진: 점심 먹고 2시 30분쯤 어때요?

민지: 좋아요. 어디서 만날까요?

우진: 1층 라운지('lounge')에서 만날까요?

Key grammatical patterns to use:

~(으)ㄴ데/는데   to explain the reason for the get-together
~(으)ㄹ래요?   to ask the other person's intention for the meeting
~(으)ㄹ까요?   to ask the other person's opinion of your choice
                        (of time and place)

[Exercise 1] Break into groups to organize the following activities. Report the arrangements you've made to the class.

(1)   주말 운동

(2)   친구 생일 파티

(3)   주말 여행

(4)   크리스마스 파티

[Exercise 2] Call the following places and set up appointments or reservations for the reasons specified.

(1)   이태리 식당: 가족들과 같이 맛있는 저녁을
                          먹고 싶어서

(2)   교수님 연구실: 모르는 것이 많아서

(3)   컴퓨터 랩: 한국어 시험이 있어서
                          연습하고 싶어서

Lesson 11 - Living in a Dormitory

CONVERSATION 1: Would you like a cup of tea?

(Woojin and Minji meet at the school cafeteria.)

Woojin:	Oh, hi, Minji! What are you up to?
Minji:	I'm just having some tea. Woojin, would you like a cup of tea?
Woojin:	Yes, please. Great, I actually wanted to have some tea.
Minji:	How's life in Korea?
Woojin:	I'm having so much fun. I've also made a lot of friends. Living in the dormitory is comfortable and fun, too.
Minji:	Woojin, do you have a single room?
Woojin:	No, I have a roommate.
Minji:	What is your roommate like?
Woojin:	He came from Australia. He really likes Korea and speaks Korean very well. He is also very kind and nice.

CONVERSATION 2: Do you want to go to see a play?

(Minji and Woojin chat in the dormitory lounge.)

Woojin:	Time flies, doesn't it? The semester's almost over already. How many courses did you take this semester?
Minji:	I took five courses.
Woojin:	You took five courses? I only took three courses.
Minji:	I was pretty busy because I had class every day, Monday through Friday. Woojin, how was your semester?
Woojin:	I was busy too because of so many assignments. I want to rest a bit starting next week.
Minji:	Hey, when we're done with exams, do you want to go to see a play?
Woonji:	Yes, it sounds good. Is there any particular play you want to see?
Minji:	Well, why don't we look for one together online?
Woojin:	Yes, let's do that.

NARRATION: Canadian student Minji

I'm a Canadian student learning Korean in Seoul. I came from Vancouver and I'm twenty-two years old. I am currently living in the school dormitory. My room number is 317 and it's the second room from the entrance. I already made a lot of friends last semester. Woojin, who lives on the third floor, is a Korean-American student. He is athletic, studious, and very kind. Woojin shares the room with Mark, a student from Australia. He is also very kind and a good-natured friend. I often have dinner together with Woojin and Mark at the dormitory cafeteria. Exams will be over next week. When they are over, we're all going to see a play together.

12과 가족 [Family]

Conversation 1 어디서 오셨어요?

(Students introduce themselves in a classroom.)

마크: 민지 씨, 어디서 오셨어요?

민지: 캐나다 밴쿠버에서 왔어요.
거기서 태어나서^{G12.1} 자랐어요.

마크: 가족들이 다 밴쿠버에 사세요?

민지: 아니요, 부모님만 거기 계시고, 형제들은
다 다른 데에 살아요.

마크: 형제가 많으세요?

민지: 네, 저까지 넷이에요.
오빠가 하나, 동생이 둘이고 제가 둘째예요.
마크 씨 가족은 어디 사세요?

마크: 부모님은 시드니에 계시고, 형은 결혼해서
미국 동부에서 살아요.
막내는 영국에서 공부하고 있는데
다음 주에 서울에 와요.

민지: 아, 그러세요?
좋겠어요.^{G12.2}

NEW WORDS

NOUN		VERB	
데	place	결혼하다	to get married
동부	East Coast	기다리다	to wait
막내	youngest child	자라다	to grow up
바지	pants	태어나다	to be born
밤	night	**ADVERB**	
부엌	kitchen	아직	still, yet
셔츠	shirt	**PARTICLE**	
형제	sibling(s)	까지	② including
PRE-NOUN		**COUNTER**	
첫	first	째/번째	ordinal numbers
ADJECTIVE		**SUFFIX**	
다르다	to be different	~겠	may, will (conjecture)
피곤하다	to be tired	~어서/아서	clausal connective (sequential)

NEW EXPRESSIONS

1. 형제 is the contracted form of 형제자매 'brothers and sisters,' meaning siblings.

2. For ordinal numbers (e.g., first, second, third), native numbers are used with the ordinal counters 번째 as in 첫 (번째) 비행기 'first flight', 두 번째 수업 'second class', 세 번째 시험 'third exam'. The ordinal counter 째 is usually used with some kinship terms such as 첫(째) 아들 'first son', 둘째 딸 'second daughter', 셋째 언니 'third older sister'.

첫(째), 첫 번째	first
둘째, 두 번째	second
셋째, 세 번째	third
넷째, 네 번째	fourth
다섯째, 다섯 번째	fifth
열째, 열 번째	tenth
스무째, 스무 번째	twentieth

Exercises

1. Fill in the blanks with your information.

저는 __LA__에서 태어났어요. 그리고 _∅ 욘스나드_에서
자랐어요. _∅ 오하이_에서 고등학교를 졸업('graduation')했어요.
대학교를 졸업하고 __LA__에서 일하고 싶어요. 그리고
결혼해서 __LA__에서 살고 싶어요.

2. Find out who has the most and fewest siblings among your classmates.
Also find whether they are the first, middle, or last child.

A: 형제가 몇 명이에요 / 어떻게 되세요?

B: 저까지 _____ 명이에요.

A: 몇 째예요?

B: [첫째, 둘째, 셋째, 막내 . . .]예요.

GRAMMAR

| G12.1 | The clausal connective ~어서/아서 (sequential) |

Examples

(1)   서점에 **가서**   I went to the bookstore, then
       사전하고 지도를 샀어요.   bought a dictionary and a map.

(2)   아침에 **일어나서** 운동했어요. I got up in the morning, then
                                    exercised.

(3)   친구를 **만나서** 저녁 먹고   I met my friend; then we had dinner
       같이 영화 보러 갔어요.   and went to see a movie together.

Notes

1. The suffix ~어서/아서 connects two clauses. It has two main functions: (a) to provide a cause-and-effect relationship between two events (G10.4) and (b) to state actions or events in chronological sequence.

> a. The function of ~어서/아서 'and so' in indicating a cause-and-effect relationship between events.

> b. ~어서/아서 '(and) then' can be used to link two sequential, tightly related events that do not have a cause-and-effect relationship, as shown in the examples.

2. ~어서/아서 clauses cannot have a past tense form of the verb. The subjects of the clauses connected by the sequential ~어서/아서 must be the same, whereas for the causal ~어서/아서, the subjects can be different.

집에 가서 잤어요.	(I) went home and (then) slept. (sequential)
날씨가 좋아서 바닷가에 놀러 갔어요.	The weather was good, (and) so (we) went to the beach to play. (causal)

3. Compare ~어서/아서 with ~고. Both forms indicate a sequence of events. However, they differ in the following ways:

~어서/아서 connects two sequential events, with the second event always a result of the first. Even when the first event does not cause the second, it is a precondition for the second event. In contrast, the basic meaning of ~고 is simply to list two or more events, and there is no implication that the first event leads to the second.

a. 친구를 만나서 영화를 보러 갔어요.	I met my friend, and (then) we went to see a movie.
b. 친구를 만나고 영화를 보러 갔어요.	I met my friend, and I went to see a movie.

In (a), when ~어서/아서 is used, it means that the speaker went to the movie with the friend. In (b), the speaker met the friend and then went to see a movie (with someone else or alone). Thus, ~고 simply lists two events without implying that they are related. Consider another pair of examples:

<table>
<tr><td>c. 백화점에 가서 선물을 샀어요.</td><td>I went to a department store and (then) bought a present (there).</td></tr>
<tr><td>d. 백화점에 가고 선물을 샀어요.</td><td>I went to a department store; I (also) bought a present (somewhere else).</td></tr>
</table>

In (c), the speaker went to a department store and bought a present there and nowhere else. In (d), when 고 is used, there is no implication that the speaker bought a present at that particular department store.

Exercises

1. Combine the two sequential events using the ~어서/아서 form, as shown in the example.

(1)   아침 6시에 일어났어요. 운동했어요.

아침 6시에 일어나서 운동했어요.

(2)   오후에 친구를 만났어요. 같이 영화 보러 갔어요.

_____

(3)   어제 옷가게에 갔어요. 셔츠하고 바지를 샀어요.

_____

(4)   의자에 앉으세요. 기다리세요.

_____

(5)   부모님께 편지를 썼어요. 부모님께 보냈어요.

_____

2. Answer the question 어제 뭐 했어요? using [place]에 가서   ~었/았어요.

(1)   A: 어제 뭐 했어요?
       B: 도서관에 가서 공부했어요.

(2)

(3)

(4)

(5)

극장-movie theatre

공원 park

G12.2   Conjectural ~겠~

Examples

(1)   A: 내일 뉴욕에서 오빠가 와요.
       B: 아, 그래요?   Is that right?
             좋**겠**어요.   (I guess that) you must be
                                      excited.
(2)   A: 어제 시험이 세 개나 있었어요.
       B: 힘들**었겠**어요.

(3)   A: 알**겠**어요?   Do you understand?
       B: a. 모르**겠**어요.   (I'm afraid that) I don't
                                      understand.

             b. 네, 알**겠**어요.   (I guess) I understand.

Notes

1. ~겠 can be used to express the speaker's guess or conjecture (and to ask the listener's guess or conjecture in questions) based on the circumstantial evidence or given information. It can be glossed in English as "I guess/ think . . ." and "You must be . . ."

> A: 점심 먹었어요?
> B: 아니요, 시간이 없어서 아직 못 먹었어요.
> A: 벌써 3시인데, 배 고프('be hungry')겠어요.

2. In making a conjecture about a past or completed event, ~었/았겠어요 is used as shown in example (2).

3. In its extended function, the conjectural suffix ~겠 can be used to raise the level of politeness. As in example (3), 알겠어요 and 모르겠어요 sound more polite than 알아요 and 몰라요.

Exercise

Comment on the following situations, using the ~겠어요 form.

> (1)   A: 어머니께서 부엌에서 갈비를 만들고 계세요.
>
>   B: (맛있다) 맛있겠어요.
>
> (2)   A: 텔레비전을 너무 많이 봤어요.
>
>   B: (머리가 아프다) _____
>
> (3)   A: 어제 밤에 세 시간밖에 못 잤어요.
>
>   B: (피곤하다) _____
>
> (4)   A: 내일 여동생이 영국에서 첫 비행기로 와요.
>
>   B: (좋다) _____
>
> (5)   A: 교통이 무척 복잡해요.
>
>   B: (학교에 늦다) _____

Conversation 2 | 가족 사진이 잘 나왔네요.

(Minji and Woojin talk about their families.)

민지: 부모님 연세가 어떻게 되세요?

우진: 아버지는 쉰다섯이시고 어머니는 쉰셋이세요.
          (taking a photo out of his bag)
          여기 우리 가족 사진이 있는데 보실래요?

민지: 어머, 사진이 참 잘 나왔네요.G12.3
          이 사진 언제 찍었어요?

우진: 작년 할머니 생신에 찍었어요.

민지: 여기 노란G12.4 한복을 입은G12.5 분이
          할머니세요?

우진: 네.

민지: 여기 키가 큰 분은 형님이시지요?

우진: 네, 우리 형이에요. 지금 대학원에 다녀요.

민지: 우진 씨가 형님이랑 눈이 닮았네요.

NEW WORDS

NOUN		ADJECTIVE	
눈	① eyes; ② snow	까맣다	to be black
		노랗다 (노란)	to be yellow
색	color (=색깔)	빨갛다	to be red
안경	eyeglasses	키가 작다	to be short
얼굴	face	키가 크다	to be tall
한복	traditional Korean dress	파랗다	to be blue
형님 *hon.*	male's older brother	하얗다	to be white
VERB		**ADVERB**	
끼다	to wear (glasses, gloves, rings)	또	and, also, too
		오래	long time
나오다	to come out	**INTERJECTION**	
다니다	to attend	어머	Oh my! Dear me!
닮다	to resemble	**SUFFIX**	
쓰다	③ to wear headgear	~네요	sentence ending indicating the speaker's reaction
입다	to wear, put on (clothes)		
PARTICLE		~(으)ㄴ	noun-modifying form (past)
(이)랑	with, and		

NEW EXPRESSIONS

1. In 우진 씨가 형님이랑 눈이 닮았어요 '(His eyes) resemble yours, Woojin', 닮았어요 is in the past-tense form but actually denotes a present state. N(이)랑 닮았다 is a pattern meaning 'to resemble N', as in 저는 엄마랑 닮았어요.

2. Colors (색/색깔):

Dictionary form	Color	Color noun
노랗다	yellow	노랑/노란색
하얗다	white	하양/하얀색
까맣다	black	까망/까만색
빨갛다	red	빨강/빨간색
파랗다	blue	파랑/파란색

More colors:

초록색	green	보라색	purple
주황색	orange	밤색	brown
분홍색	pink	회색	gray

3. The particle (이)랑 is more casual than the particle 하고.

4. Clothing:

Korean has different verbs for 'to put on, wear,' depending on how the item is worn.

Item		to put on, wear	to take off
옷	clothes	입다 (apparel other than headgear, footwear, gloves)	벗다
셔츠	shirts		
치마	skirts		
바지	pants/trousers		
모자	hats, caps	쓰다 (headgear)	벗다
안경	eyeglasses	쓰다/끼다	벗다
신(발)	footwear	신다 (footwear)	벗다
운동화	sneakers		
양말	socks/stockings		
장갑	gloves	끼다 (things that fit tightly)	벗다 (gloves)
반지	rings		빼다 (rings)
목걸이	necklaces	하다	빼다
귀걸이	earrings		
시계	wristwatches	차다	풀다
벨트	belts	하다/매다	풀다
넥타이	ties		
가방	backpacks/purses	메다/들다	

Note that the verb 하다 can be used with necklaces, earrings, and other accessories except 시계.

Exercises

1. Fill in the blanks with the color terms.

    (1)   머리: <u>까만색</u>

    (2)   눈: _____

    (3)   바지: _____

    (4)   가방: _____

    (5)   좋아하는 색깔: _____

    (6)   자주 입는 옷 색깔: _____

2. Connect the corresponding nouns and predicates.

사진을 •	• 다녀요.
옷을 •	• 닮았어요.
형제가 •	• 찍어요.
대학원에 •	• 와요.
눈이 •	• 입어요.

3. Fill in the blanks with your information.

    (1)   저는 _____(이)랑 눈이 닮았어요.

    (2)   저는 _____(이)랑 얼굴이 닮았어요.

    (3)   저는 _____(이)랑 성격('personality')이 닮았어요.

    (4)   저는 아버지/어머니랑 _____이/가 닮았어요.

4. Fill in the blanks with the appropriate clothing/accessory items.

    (1)   _____을/를 입어요

    (2)   _____을/를 신어요.

    (3)   _____을/를 써요

    (4)   _____을/를 해요.

5. Describe what you are wearing.

Example: 저는 하얀 셔츠에 파란 바지를 입고
안경을 썼어요.

6. Find out the following information.

(1)   오늘 청바지를 입은 사람이 누구예요?

(2)   오늘 모자를 쓴 사람이 있어요? 무슨 색 모자를 썼어요?

(3)   교실에 안경을 낀 사람이 몇 명 있어요?

(4)   학생들이 좋아하는 셔츠 색이 뭐예요?

GRAMMAR

G12.3   The sentence ending ~네요

Examples

(1)   저기 스티브가 **오네요**.   Steve is coming there.

(2)   A: 미국에서 얼마나 살았어요?   How long have you lived in
                                        the United States?
       B: 15년 살았어요.   I have lived (in the United
                                        States) for fifteen years.
       A: 미국에서 오래 **살았네요**.   You have lived in the United
                                        States for a long time.

(3)   A: 어제 밤 2시까지 공부했어요.   I studied until 2 a.m. last
                                        night.
       B: 피곤**하겠네요**.   You must be tired.

Notes

1. The sentence ending ~네요 expresses the speaker's spontaneous reaction (such as surprise, admiration, or sympathy) to some new information.

2. Compare ~네요 with ~어요/아요. ~어요/아요 is simply informative; ~네요 also carries the speaker's emotion, which is frequently contrary to what the speaker had been expecting. For example, compare the two sentences below:

> a. 소피아가 벌써 학교에 갔어요.   Sophia already went to school.
> b. 소피아가 벌써 학교에 갔네요.   (To my surprise) Sophia already went to school.

The speaker in (b) was thinking that Sophia had not gone to school yet, but finds that she has. Thus, ~네요 is used when expectations conflict with facts, causing surprise (or some other feeling).

3. The conjecture suffix ~겠 and the ending ~네요 can be combined to express the speaker's realization of what would happen to the given input. In (3), the meaning of 피곤하겠네요 is '[I guess] you must be tired!' and speaker B says this in reaction to what speaker A said about himself.

Exercise

Change the following sentence endings into the ~네요 form, as in the example.

> (1)   오늘 날씨가 아주 더워요.   오늘 날씨가 아주 덥네요.
>
> (2)   옷이 참 예뻐요.   _____
>
> (3)   제 안경이 여기 있어요.   _____
>
> (4)   마크가 아직 집에 안 왔어요.   _____
>
> (5)   시험이 어려워요.   _____
>
> (6)   바지가 너무 커요.   _____
>
> (7)   제니는 키가 작아요.   _____

G12.4 Irregular predicates with /ㅎ/

Examples

(1)	저는 **노란** 색을 좋아해요.	I like the color yellow.
(2)	**이런** 모자는 **어때요?**	How about this kind of hat?
(3)	제 머리는 **까매요.**	My hair is black.

Notes

1. Some adjective stems ending in the consonant /ㅎ/ drop the stem-final /ㅎ/ before a vowel. This irregular pattern applies mostly to color terms and demonstrative adjectives such as 이렇다/그렇다/저렇다 'to be this/ that way'. The irregular pattern is illustrated below with 노랗다 'to be yellow'.

노랗 + ~은	→	노란
노랗 + ~아요	→	노래요
노랗 + ~아서	→	노래서
노랗 + ~을까요?	→	노랄까요?
노랗 + ~았어요	→	노랬어요

/ㅎ/ does not drop before the deferential ending, as in 노랗습니다, because the ending ~습니다 begins with a consonant. Observe more examples of these irregular adjectives.

Dictionary form		~습니다/ ㅂ니다	~어요/ 아요	~ㄴ/은	~세요/ 으세요
빨갛다	to be red	빨갛습니다	빨개요	빨간	—
하얗다	to be white	하얗습니다	하애요	하얀	—
까맣다	to be black	까맣습니다	까매요	까만	—
이렇다	to be this way	이렇습니다	이래요	이런	이러세요
그렇다	to be so	그렇습니다	그래요	그런	그러세요
저렇다	to be that way	저렇습니다	저래요	저런	저러세요
어떻다	to be some way	어떻습니까	어때요	어떤	어떠세요

2. Some stems, such as 좋다, 많다, and 싫다 ('to be undesirable'), follow the regular pattern of conjugation: 좋습니다, 좋아요, 좋은.

Exercise

Conjugate the given dictionary forms according to the context.

(1) 저는 머리가 (좋다) <u>좋은</u> 사람하고 결혼하고 싶어요.

(2) 마크 눈은 (파랗다)_____ 색이에요.

(3) 동생이 머리가 (까맣다)_____.

(4) 그 남자는 (어떻다)_____ 사람이에요?

(5) 김 선생님이 (어떻다) _____ ?

(6) 요즘은 (많다)_____ 학생들이 한국어를 배워요.

| G12.5 | The noun-modifying form [Verb ~(으)ㄴ] + N (past) |

Examples

(1) 어제 **먹은** 갈비가 맛있었어요.   The *kalbi* that I ate yesterday was tasty.

(2) 스티브가 **입은** 옷은 아주 비싸요.   The clothes that Steve is wearing are very expensive.

(3) 어제 **만난** 친구를 오늘 또 만났어요.   Today I saw the friend again whom I (had) met yesterday.

Notes

1. [Verb stem~(으)ㄴ] + N is the past form of a verb in relative clauses (noun-modifying constructions). Recall that when ~(으)ㄴ occurs with adjectives, it indicates a present situation (G9.2).

a. 민지가 **산** 차는 작아요.   The car that Minji **bough**t is small.

b. 민지가 **작은** 차를 샀어요.   Minji bought a **small** car.

[~(으)ㄴ] + N, (a) when used with verbs, expresses past or completed actions or events (see G10.5 for the use of ~는 for present or ongoing action), but (b) when used with adjectives, expresses present situations.

2. When verbs for 'to wear, put on' occur with ~(으)ㄴ, they indicate the result of a past action. For example:

a.	[모자를 쓴] 사람은 우리 남동생이에요.	The person who wears a cap is my younger brother.
b.	[안경을 낀] 사람은 우리 형이에요.	The person who wears glasses is my older brother.

3. Conjugation of noun-modifying constructions:

	Verb	Adjective	있다/없다	이다
Past/ completed	(으)ㄴ	-	-	-
Present/ ongoing	는	(으)ㄴ	는	ㄴ
Prospective/ unrealized	(으)ㄹ	(으)ㄹ	을	ㄹ

Notice that past/complete suffixes do not occur with adjectives (including 있다/없다 and 이다).

Examples of conjugation:

	Verb	Adjective	있다/없다	이다
	읽다 가다	좋다 싸다	재미있다 맛없다	학생이다
Past/ completed	읽은 간	-	-	-
Present/ ongoing	읽는 가는	좋은 싼	재미있는 맛없는	학생인
Prospective/ unrealized	읽을 갈	좋을 쌀	재미있을 맛없을	학생일

Exercises

1. Underline the noun-modifying (relative) clause in each sentence below, and then translate the whole sentence into English as in (1).

(1)   이게 제가 지난 주에 <u>읽은</u> 책이에요.

   <u>This is the book that I read last week.</u>

(2)   이건 어제 마크한테서 <u>받은</u> 선물이에요.

   _____

(3)   우리 어머니가 <u>만든</u> 음식은 맛있어요.

   _____

(4)   지난 학기에 한국어를 <u>가르치신</u> 분은 이민수 선생님이에요.

   _____

(5)   스티브가 서울에서 <u>찍은</u> 사진들이 여기 있습니다.

   _____

(6)   키가 크고 안경을 <u>낀</u> 남자는 누구예요?

   _____

2. Change the verbs in the following noun-modifying clauses using the past-tense form ~(으)ㄴ, and then translate the clauses into English.

(1)   스티브가 **읽는** 책   <u>the book (that) Steve reads</u>
   <u>스티브가 **읽은** 책</u>   <u>the book (that) Steve read</u>

(2)   동생한테 주는 선물   _____
   동생한테 준 선물

(3)   내가 듣는 음악   _____
   내가 들은 음악

(4)   마크가 쓰는 편지   _____
   마크가 쓴 편지

(5)   유미가 마시는 커피 _____

유미가 _마신 커피_____

3. Make sentences using the noun-modifying clauses you made in exercise 2.

> Example: 스티브가 읽은 책
>   → 스티브가 읽은 책은 재미있었습니다.

Narration 가족 사진

우리 가족은 할머니, 아버지, 어머니, 누나, 형, 남동생, 그리고 나, 모두 일곱 명입니다. 여기 우리 가족 사진이 있습니다. 이 가족 사진은 작년 할머니 생신에 찍은 사진입니다. 가운데 노란 한복을 입고 계신 분이 할머니이십니다. 할머니는 연세가 많으신데 아주 건강하십니다. 할머니 뒤에 계신 분들이 우리 부모님이십니다. 키가 크고 안경을 낀 사람은 우리 형입니다. 형은 대학원에 다닙니다. 머리가 긴 여자는 우리 누나입니다. 누나는 지난 봄에 결혼해서 지금은 미국 동부에서 살고 있습니다. 파란 모자를 쓴 남자는 제 남동생입니다. 남동생은 지금 고등학교[1]에 다닙니다. 내년에 대학생이 됩니다.

1. 고등학교: high school

봄 - spring

Exercises

1. Answer the following questions based on the narration.

(1)   우진의 가족은 모두 몇 명입니까?   *일곱*

(2)   이 가족 사진은 언제 찍은 것입니까?   *전역*

(3)   할머니는 무슨 옷을 입고 계십니까?   *노란 한복*

(4)   사진에서 부모님은 어디에 계십니까?   *뒤에 계세요*

(5)   형은 어떤 사람입니까?   *대학교 새원생이에요*

(6)   누나는 어떤 사람입니까?   *결혼 안한 사람이에요 운이세요*

(7)   남동생은 어떤 사람입니까?   *고등학생입니다*

2. Ask your classmate to read the narration; then, based on what you hear, draw a family photo with your book closed.

CULTURE

1. 아름다운 한복 (Beautiful *hanbok*)

한복 is a term collectively used for traditional Korean clothes. These are often characterized as a set of colorful garments with simple lines that don't have any pockets. Although 한복 literally means "Korean clothing," 한복 today particularly refers to the clothing of the Joseon dynasty. Typically, women wear a wrap-around skirt (치마) and men wear roomy pants bound at the ankle (바지). 저고리, an upper garment with a ribbon to tie in the front, was worn by both women and men. With the developments in textiles as well as changes in society, a wide selection of fabrics became available to make 한복—from ramie and cotton to silk. Modern modification also brought pockets, zippers, and other diverse changes to 한복. Nowadays,

people usually wear 한복 only on special occasions such as weddings or traditional holidays.

2. 호칭 (Extending family terms to other social relations)

In Korean, some family terms are often extended to refer to social relations without blood ties. An elder male is addressed 할아버지 (grandfather); an elder female, 할머니 (grandmother); a middle-aged male, 아저씨 (uncle); and a middle-aged female, 아주머니 (aunt).

Among group members of similar age, terms referring to siblings are used. 언니 is a term a younger female uses to address an older female, while 오빠 is a term a younger female uses to address an older male. 누나 is used by a younger male to refer to an older female, while 형 is used by a younger male to refer to an older male.

To address the father of your friend, you can say 아버님, an honorific expression meaning one's father. To address the mother of your friend, you can say either 어머님 or 어머니, both of which are honorific expressions meaning one's mother.

USAGE

A. Talking about family

가족	이름	나이	사는 곳 (residence)
할머니	김순아	75	로스앤젤레스
아버지	한갑수	53	로스앤젤레스
어머니	이남희	49	로스앤젤레스
누나	한유경	24	프린스턴
형	한준호	22	텍사스
나	한유진	20	서울
여동생	한미선	17	로스앤젤레스

[Exercise 1] The chart above lists ages and places of residence for each of Yujin's family members. Work in pairs to exchange information on each of Yujin's family members.

Example:　A:　유진 씨 할머니 연세는 어떻게 되세요?
　　　　　B:　여든 다섯이세요.
　　　　　A:　지금 어디 사세요?
　　　　　B:　로스앤젤레스에 사세요.

[Exercise 2] Answer the following questions:

(1)　유진은 집에서 몇 째예요?
　　　(몇 째 [order of birth among siblings])
(2)　막내의 이름은 뭐예요?
(3)　아들이 몇 명 있어요? 딸은 몇 명이에요?
(4)　누나는 이름이 뭐예요? 어디서 살아요?
(5)　할머님 성함은 어떻게 되세요?

[Exercise 3] Practice the following dialogue:

A:　가족이 많으세요?
B:　네, 할아버지, 아버지, 어머니, 언니, 오빠, 여동생, 그리고 나,
　　모두 7명이에요.
A:　부모님은 어디 사세요?
B:　보스톤에 사세요.
A:　형제들은 다 어디 살아요?
B:　오빠는 뉴욕에 살고, 언니는 하와이에 살고, 여동생은
　　보스톤에 살아요.

Now play the role of speaker B and describe your own family.

A:　가족이 많으세요?
B:　네, _____
　　(아니요, _____ 밖에 없어요.)

A: 부모님은 어디 사세요?

B: _____에 사세요.

A: 형제들은 다 어디 살아요?

B: _____

[Exercise 4] Draw your family tree including your grandparents, parents, and siblings, and tell your classmates about the people on it.

B. Ordinal numbers

For the order of lessons (lesson 1, lesson 2, etc.), Sino-Korean numbers are used: 일 과, 이 과, 삼 과, 사 과, and so on.

[Exercise 1] Answer the following questions:

(1)   오늘 몇 과를 공부해요? _____

(2)   어제는 몇 과를 공부했어요? _____

(3)   내일 몇 과를 배워요? _____

[Exercise 2] Using the images in the boxes below, answer the questions.

1st	2nd	3rd	4th	5th	6th	7th

(1)   사전이 어디 있어요?   일곱 번째 박스('box')에 있어요.

(2)   한국어 책은 어디 있어요?   _____

(3)   연필은 어디 있어요?   _____

(4)   가방은 어디 있어요?   _____

(5)   세 번째에는 뭐가 있어요?   _____

(6)   다섯 번째에는 뭐가 있어요? _____

(7)   두 번째에는 뭐가 있어요?   _____

황 생 - peachish brown/polyelshin

C. Describing clothes

[Exercise] Describe the clothes the family members in the picture are wearing, as well as the non-clothing items they may have.

할머니는 한복을 <u>입으셨어요</u>.

아버지는 넥타이를 _____

어머니는 가방을 _____

형은 안경을 _____

동생은 모자를 _____

누나는 치마를 _____

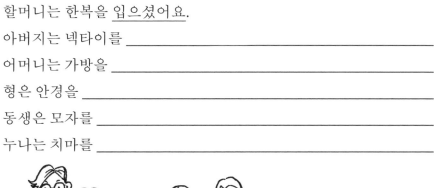

D. Describing colors

Notice the difference between color adjectives and their conjugated forms.
우리 어머니 눈은 까만 색이에요. 어머니 머리도 까매요.

[Exercise] Based on your own appearance, answer the following questions in Korean.

(1)   머리가 무슨 색이에요? _____

(2)   눈은 무슨 색깔이에요? _____

(3)   좋아하는 색이 뭐예요? _____

(4)   오늘 입은 옷 색깔이 뭐예요? _____

(5)   무슨 색 옷을 자주 입어요? _____

Lesson 12 - Family

CONVERSATION 1: Where are you from?
(Students introduce themselves in a classroom.)

Mark:	Minji, where are you from?
Minji:	Vancouver, Canada. I was born and raised there.
Mark:	Does everyone in your family live in Vancouver?
Minji:	No, only my parents live there; my siblings live elsewhere.
Mark:	Do you have many siblings?
Minji:	Yes, there are four of us. I have one older brother and two younger siblings. I'm the second child. Mark, where does your family live?
Mark:	My parents live in Sydney. My older brother has lived in the United States on the East Coast since he married. The youngest, who is studying in England, will come to Seoul next week.
Minji:	Oh, really? You must be excited.

CONVERSATION 2: Your family photo came out well.
(Minji and Woojin talk about their families.)

Minji:	How old are your parents?
Woojin:	My father is fifty-five years old and my mother is fifty-three years old.
	(taking a photo from his bag)
	Would you like to see my family photo?
Minji:	Oh, it came out really well. When was this taken?
Woojin:	This was taken last year on my grandmother's birthday.
Minji:	Is your grandmother the one with a yellow *hanbok*?
Woojin:	Yes.
Miniji:	Is the tall person your brother?
Woojin:	Yes, that's my brother. He's in graduate school now.
Minij:	Your eyes resemble his.

NARRATION: Family photo

There are seven of us in my family: my grandmother, father, mother, an older sister, an older brother, a younger brother, and me. This is our family photo. This photo was taken a year ago on my grandmother's birthday. The person in the middle wearing a yellow *hanbok* is my grandmother. She is quite healthy for her age. The couple behind my grandmother is my parents. The tall person with glasses is my older brother. He goes to graduate school. The girl with long hair is my older sister. She got married last spring and now lives in the United States on the East Coast. The boy wearing a blue baseball cap is my younger brother. He's in high school. He will be in college next year.

13과 전화   [On the Telephone]

Conversation 1	스티브 씨 좀 바꿔 주세요.

(Soobin calls Steve to find out why he was absent.

(따르릉 따르릉)

스티브: 여보세요.

수빈: 거기 스티브 씨 집이지요?

스티브: 네, 그런데요.

수빈: 스티브 씨 좀 바꿔 주세요.^{G13.1}

스티브: 전데요. 실례지만 누구세요?

수빈: 저 김수빈이에요. 오늘 왜 학교에 안 왔어요?

스티브: 감기에 걸려서 못 갔어요.

수빈: 많이 아파요?

스티브: 아침엔 많이 아팠는데, 이젠 좀 괜찮아요.

수빈: 내일은 학교에 올 거예요?

스티브: 네, 시험이 있어서 가야 돼요.^{G13.2}

수빈: 그래요? 그럼 몸조리 잘 하세요.

스티브: 네, 전화 주셔서 감사합니다.

수빈: 그럼 또 전화할게요.^{G13.3}

NEW WORDS

NOUN		ADJECTIVE	
도시	city	배(가) 고프다	to be hungry
몸조리	care of health	**ADVERB**	
엄마	mom	나중에	later
VERB		다시	again
감기에 걸리다	to have/catch a cold	여보세요	hello (on the phone)
돕다	to help	이따가	a little later
바꾸다	to change, switch	이젠	now (이제+는)
빨래하다	to do the laundry	**SUFFIX**	
부치다	to mail (a letter, parcel)	~(으)ㄹ게요	I will (volition or promise)
비(가) 오다	to rain	~어/아 주다	do something for another's benefit
빌리다	to borrow		
빌려주다	to lend	~어/아야 되다	must (obligation or necessity)
실례하다	to be excused		

NEW EXPRESSIONS

1. 따르릉 따르릉 is an onomatopoeic expression denoting the telephone ring.

2. 여보세요 'hello' (for telephone) comes from 여기 보세요 'Look here'.

3. 실례지만 누구세요? 'Excuse me, but who is this?' 실례지만 'excuse me, but' can precede a question to express courtesy. Note that 'Excuse me' is 실례합니다.

> 저어, 실례지만 지금 몇 시예요?
> 저어, 실례지만 말씀 좀 묻겠습니다.

4. Both 지금 and 이제 (이젠) indicate the present moment of speech and can be translated as 'now'. However, the two expressions refer to the present moment in two different senses. 이제 involves a change in situation from the previous moments, whereas 지금 simply indicates the present moment without relating it to any other time.

5. 몸조리 잘 하세요 'Please take good care of yourself' is an idiomatic expression addressed to someone who is ill. 몸 is 'body' and 조리 is 'care of health, recuperation'.

6. Some telephone expressions:

전화번호	telephone number
여보세요.	Hello.
[person]한테 전화하세요.	Please call [a person].
전화해 주세요.	Please give me a call.
[person]한테서 전화가 오다.	The phone call is from [a person].
전화 받으세요.	Please answer the phone.
[person] 좀 바꿔 주세요.	May I speak to [a person]?
잠깐만 기다리세요.	Just a minute, please.
이따가 다시 전화할게요.	I will call you later.

7. Parts of the body:

얼굴	face
입술	lips
가슴	chest
등	back
키	height
머리	head/hair
눈	eye
귀	ear
코	nose
입	mouth
이	tooth
턱	chin
목	neck
어깨	shoulder
팔	arm
손	hand
배	stomach, abdomen
허리	waist
다리	leg
발	foot

Exercise

Complete the following telephone dialogue between Steve and Minji.

<table>
<tr><td></td><td>(ring ring)</td></tr>
<tr><td>스티브:</td><td>_____ (hello).</td></tr>
<tr><td>민지:</td><td>_____ (hello).</td></tr>
<tr><td></td><td>거기 스티브 씨 집이지요?</td></tr>
<tr><td>스티브:</td><td>네, 그런데요.</td></tr>
<tr><td>민지:</td><td>스티브 씨 있어요?</td></tr>
<tr><td>스티브:</td><td>전데요.</td></tr>
<tr><td></td><td>_____(excuse me but . . .) 누구세요?</td></tr>
<tr><td>민지:</td><td>저 민지인데요. 오늘 수업에 왜 안 왔어요?</td></tr>
<tr><td>스티브:</td><td>감기에 _____ 못 갔어요.</td></tr>
<tr><td></td><td>(I couldn't go because I had a cold.)</td></tr>
<tr><td>민지:</td><td>그래요? 그럼 몸조리 잘 하세요.</td></tr>
</table>

GRAMMAR

G13.1 The benefactive expression ~어/아 주다

Examples

(1) 파티에 **와 주세요**.   Please come to the party.

(2) 엄마가 저한테 차를 **사 주셨어요**   Mom bought me a car.

(3) A: 제 전화 번호 알아요?   Do you know my phone number?

   B: 아니요, 번호 좀 **가르쳐 주세요**.   No, please let me have it.

(4) **도와 주셔서** 감사합니다.   Thank you for helping (me).

Notes

1. 주다 as a main verb means 'to give', as in the following examples:

마이클이 리사한테 꽃을 주었어요.   선생님이 저한테 사전을 주셨어요.

The recipient is marked with the particle 한테 or 에게.

2. As an auxiliary verb, 주다 is used in the construction of [verb stem + ~어/아 주다] which means 'to do something for someone'. Compare the two sentences below:

(a)   스티브가 책을 읽었어요.
(b)   스티브가 동생한테 책을 읽어 주었어요.

Sentence (a) simply means that Steve read a book, but (b) means that Steve read a book to someone else.

[Verb stem + ~어/아 주다] takes the following forms:

사 주다   to buy for someone's benefit
읽어 주다   to read for someone's benefit
빌려 주다*   to lend for someone's benefit
도와 주다   to help for someone's benefit

*빌려 주다 'to lend' (c.f. 빌리다 'to borrow')

3. ~어/아 주세요 is also used when requesting something in which the benefit is for the speaker: "Please do . . . for me."

a.   책을 읽으세요.   Read the book.
b.   책을 (저한테) 읽어 주세요.   Please read the book (for me).

Both ~어/아 주세요 and ~(으)세요 can be used in making requests or commands. However, they differ in degree of politeness. ~어/아 주세요 is much more polite than ~(으)세요. Sentence (a) simply imposes some action on the listener, whereas (b) indicates that the speaker is making the request for his/her own benefit. When you are asking to speak to someone on the phone, ___ 씨 좀 바꾸세요 is not appropriate. Instead, use ____씨 좀 바꿔 주세요.

4. ~어/아 주셔서 감사합니다 is used to express gratitude. The adverb 대단히 'very much' can be added. 감사합니다 can be replaced with 고맙습니다.

생일 파티에 와 주셔서 감사합니다/고맙습니다.	Thank you for coming to my birthday party.
한국어를 가르쳐 주셔서 감사합니다/고맙습니다.	Thank you for teaching me Korean.

Compare ~어/아 주다 with other sentence endings below. Notice that when the stem 주 is followed by ~어요, the contracted form 줘요 can be used.

Dictionary form	~어/아요	~(으)세요	~어/아 줘요	~어/아 주세요
오다	와요	오세요	와 줘요	와 주세요
가르치다	가르쳐요	가르치세요	가르쳐 줘요	가르쳐 주세요
읽다	읽어요	읽으세요	읽어 줘요	읽어 주세요
전화하다	전화해요	전화하세요	전화해 줘요	전화해 주세요
쓰다	써요	쓰세요	써 줘요	써 주세요
돕다	도와요	도우세요	도와 줘요	도와 주세요

| G13.2 | Expressing obligation or necessity: ~어/아야 되다 |

Examples

(1)   매일 운동해**야 돼요**.   (We/I) have to exercise every day.

(2)   내일 아침 교수님하고   I have an appointment with my
       약속이 있어요.   professor tomorrow morning.
       일찍 일어나**야 돼요**.   I have to get up early.

(3)   A: 이번 주말에 바빠요?
       B: 네, 집 청소하고 빨래해**야 돼요**.

(4)   A: 오후에 뭐 할 거예요?
       B: 도서관에 가서 책을 빌려**야 돼요**.

Notes

1. ~어/아야 되다 and its alternative form ~어/아야 하다 express the idea of obligation or necessity. ~어/아야 하다 sounds slightly more formal than ~어/아야 되다.

학생은 열심히 공부해야 돼요.   Students must study hard.
                               (colloquial)
학생은 열심히 공부해야 해요.   Students must study hard.
                               (slightly formal)

2. ~어/아야 되다 and ~어/아야 하다 occur in the following forms:

좋다	좋아야 돼요/해요	have to be good
가다	가야 돼요/해요	have to go
먹다	먹어야 돼요/해요	have to eat
모자를 쓰다	모자를 써야 돼요/해요	have to wear a hat
조용하다	조용해야 돼요/해요	have to be quiet
학생이다	학생이어야 돼요/해요	have to be a student

Exercises

1. Change the verbs in parentheses to express necessity by using ~어/아야 되다.

> (1)   비가 와요. 우산을 (사다) <u>사야 돼요</u>.
>
> (2)   배가 고파요. 식당에 (가다) _____.
>
> (3)   도시에서는 차가 많이 막혀서 지하철을 (타다) _____.
>
> (4)   돈이 없어요. 일을 (하다) _____.
>
> (5)   다음 학기에는 심리학 수업을 (듣다) _____.
>
> (6)   룸메이트를 찾아요. 그런데 학생 (이다) _____.

2. Tell your class what you need to do this week, using ~어/아야 되다 as in the example.

> 월요일: 시험   <u>월요일에는 시험을 봐야 돼요</u>.
>
> 화요일: 수업   _____
>
> 수요일: 한국어 숙제   _____
>
> 목요일: 친구   _____
>
> 금요일: 생일 파티   _____
>
> 토요일: 집 청소   _____

G13.3	The sentence ending ~(으)ㄹ게요

Examples

(1)	A:	전화 왔는데 제가 받을까요?	The telephone is ringing; shall I answer it?
	B:	괜찮아요. 제가 **받을게요**.	It's all right. I will answer it.

(2)   A: 지금 시간 있으세요?   Do you have time now?
       B: 지금 좀 바쁜데요.   I'm a little busy now.
       A: 그럼, 이따가 다시 **올게요**. Then I will come again
                                            later.

Notes

1. The sentence ending ~(으)ㄹ게요 expresses the speaker's willingness, assurance, or promise to do something for the listener's sake. This form can be used only in statements, not in questions. The subject must be in the first person.

2. Compare ~(으)ㄹ게요 and ~(으)ㄹ래요 (G11.2). Neither ~(으)ㄹ게요 nor ~(으)ㄹ래요 allows a third person to be the subject of the sentence. Unlike ~(으)ㄹ게요, ~(으)ㄹ래요 can be used in questions, in which case the listener's intention is being asked.

3. While ~(으)ㄹ게요 denotes willingness, assurance, or promise, ~(으)ㄹ래요 denotes intention and assertion. Compare these examples:

[교실에서]

선생님: 누가 책을 읽을래요?   Who will read the book?
스티브: 제가 읽을게요.   I will read it. (volunteering)
마크: 아니에요, 제가 읽을래요.   No, I will read it. (asserting)

[식당에서]

A: 뭐 드시겠어요?   What would you like to eat?
B: 저는 갈비 먹을게요.   I will have *kalbi*. (modest, guest-like)
C: 저는 불고기 먹을래요.   I will have *pulgogi*. (asserting)

Exercise

Complete the following dialogue by conjugating the verbs using the ~(으)ㄹ게요 form.

(1) A: 내일 몇 시에 만날까요?

B: 제가 오늘 밤에 (전화하다) 전화할게요.

(2) A: 숙제를 하는데 너무 어려워요.

B: 제가 도와 (주다) _____.

(3) A: 오늘 집에 일찍 오세요.

B: 네, 일찍 (오다) _____.

(4) A: 지금 커피 마실래요?

B: 아니에요. 괜찮아요. 나중에 (마시다) _____.

(5) A: 음식이 없어요. 누가 장보러 갈래요?

B: 제가 (가다) _____.

Conversation 2 박 교수님 댁이지요?

(Mark calls Professor Park, and his wife answers the phone.)

(따르릉 따르릉)

사모님: 여보세요.

마크: 여보세요. 거기 박 교수님 댁이지요?

사모님: 네, 그런데요.

마크: 박 교수님 좀 부탁합니다.

사모님: 네, 잠깐만 기다리세요.
            여보, 전화 받으세요.

박 교수님: 여보세요. 전화 바꿨습니다.

마크: 저, 마크 스미스인데요,
            한국어 수업 때문에[G13.4] 좀 뵙고 싶은데
            내일 학교에 나오세요?

박 교수님: 네, 오후 2시부터 4시까지 연구실에 있을
            거예요.

마크: 그럼 2시 반에 연구실로 가겠습니다.[G13.5]

박 교수님: 그럼 내일 봐요.

마크: 네, 안녕히 계세요.

NEW WORDS

NOUN		ADJECTIVE	
그동안	meantime	시끄럽다	to be noisy
뉴스	news	**VERB**	
메시지	message	남기다	to leave (a message)
물가	cost of living	돈이 들다	to cost money
반	half (e.g., 30 min)	들어가다	to enter
발	foot	부탁하다	to ask a favor
비	rain	**ADVERB**	
사모님 *hon.*	someone's wife	그만	without doing anything further
신발	shoes		
여보	honey, dear	때문에	because of
인터뷰	interview	잠깐만	for a short time
PRE-NOUN		**SUFFIX**	
새	new	~겠	would (intention)

NEW EXPRESSIONS

1. . . . 좀 부탁합니다 (lit. I would like to ask you a favor) is used in telephone conversations to ask "May I speak to . . .?"

2. 여보 'honey, darling' is used exclusively between husbands and wives.

3. 전화 바꿨습니다 (lit. I switched the telephone) is a standard expression to report to the caller that the requested person has taken over the receiver from another person.

4. 좀 뵙고 싶은데요 'I would like to see you' is used only to a senior person or a distant adult.

Exercise

Make up a telephone dialogue with your partner by changing the underlined portions of the example.

    (1)   A: 여보세요, 거기 <u>식당</u>이지요?
                 B: 네, 그런데요.

A: <u>이민수 씨</u> 좀 부탁합니다.
B: 실례지만 누구세요?
A: 네, [your name]인데요.
B: 잠깐만 기다리세요.

(2)   꽃집/ 김상호
(3)   커피숍/ 이미진
(4)   극장/ 신성희
(5)   연구실/ 박영진 교수님
(6)   서울은행/ 장윤진
(7)   마크 씨 집/ 마크

GRAMMAR

G13.4 Noun 때문에

Examples

(1)   A: 그동안 어떻게 지내셨어요?
       B: 한국어 **수업 때문에** 좀 바빴어요.

(2)   A: **룸메이트 때문에** 못 잤어요.
       B: 피곤하겠어요.

(3)   감기 **때문에** 어제 집에 일찍 들어갔어요.

Notes

1. The word 때문 means 'reason'. It cannot be used by itself, but must be preceded by a noun or noun phrase. With a preceding noun and the particle 에, the construction [Noun 때문에] expresses a causal relationship as in "because of."

2. After [Noun 때문에] the main predicate may be omitted to avoid repetition.

A: 한국에 왜 가세요?

B: 일 때문에 가요 or 일 때문에요.

Exercises

1. Make complete sentences using 때문에, as shown in the example.

(1)	숙제 / 시간이 없어요.	숙제 때문에 시간이 없어요.
(2)	한국어 수업 / 학교에 일찍 와요.	_____
(3)	비 / 차가 많이 막혔어요.	_____
(4)	여자친구/ 돈이 많이 들어요.	_____
(5)	작은 신발 / 발이 아파요.	_____
(6)	인터뷰 / 새 옷을 샀어요.	_____

2. Answer the following questions using the [Noun 때문에] or [Noun 때문에요] construction.

(1)	요즘 왜 바쁘세요?	[시험]
(2)	왜 기숙사에서 나왔어요?	[시끄러운 룸메이트]
(3)	왜 머리가 아파요?	[감기]
(4)	어제 왜 학교에 안 왔어요?	[한국에서 온 친구]
(5)	왜 돈이 많이 들어요?	[비싼 물가]

G13.5 Intentional ~겠~

Examples

(1)   저는 내일 가**겠**습니다.   I will go tomorrow.

(2)   A: 뭐 마시**겠**어요?   What would you like to drink?

       B: 커피 마실게요.   Coffee, please.

(3)   A: 누가 책을 읽**겠**어요?   Who will read the book?
       B: 제가 읽**겠**습니다.   I will read it.

(4)   A: 거기 이 선생님 계세요?
       B: 지금 안 계시는데요. 메시지를 남기**겠**습니까?

Notes

1. ~겠~, which indicates conjecture (G12.2), can also be used to express
the speaker's intention or volition, and can be glossed as 'will'. In speech,
~(으)ㄹ래요 usually replaces intentional ~겠~ which cannot be preceded
by the past-tense suffix ~었/았 while conjectural ~겠~ (G12.2) can.
Intentional ~겠~ indicates the speaker's intention or volition in statements
and probes for that of the listener in questions.

    Statements:
    제가 가겠어요.   I will go.
    내일 다시 오겠어요.   I will come again tomorrow.

    On the street
    말씀 좀 묻겠습니다.   May I ask you something?
                                       (lit. I will ask you something.)

    Greeting
    처음 뵙겠습니다.   Nice to meet you. (lit. I'm meeting
                                       you for the first time.)

    Questions:
    At a restaurant
    뭐 드시겠어요?   What would you like to eat?

2. In addition, ~겠~ occurs in idiomatic expressions in the following
contexts:

    Saying good-bye
    그만 가 보겠습니다.   See you later.
                                       (lit. I'll be leaving now.)

    Before a meal
    잘 먹겠습니다.   I will enjoy the meal.
                                       (lit. I will eat well.)

In a classroom

시험을 시작하겠습니다.   We will begin the exam.

Weather forecast

내일은 비가 오겠습니다.   It will rain tomorrow.

News report

지금부터 뉴스를   The news will start now.
시작하겠습니다.

Exercise

Translate the following sentences using ~겠~.

    (1)   (On the street) May I ask you something?

        _____

    (2)   Nice to meet you.

        _____

    (3)   A: Who will read lesson 11?

        _____

        B: I will read it.

        _____

    (4)   (To a professor) I will come to your office tomorrow at
        9 o'clock.

        _____

Narration 전화 메시지

1. (Steve leaves a voice message on Mark's phone.)

마크 씨, 안녕하세요? 저 스티브
윌슨인데요. 한국어 숙제 때문에
전화했어요. 내일 아침 10시에
학교 도서관 앞에서 만나고 싶은데,
시간이 괜찮아요? 저한테 전화 좀
해 주세요. 제 전화 번호는
512-6094예요. 안녕히 계세요.

2. (Minji leaves a voice message on her mom's phone.)

엄마, 저 민지예요. 그동안 잘
지내셨지요? 저는 학교에 잘 다니고
있어요. 저어, 책을 사야 되는데
지난 달에 받은 돈을 다 썼어요.
서울은 물가가 비싸서 돈이 굉장히
많이 들어요. 죄송하지만, 은행으로
돈 좀 부쳐 주세요. 오백 불만 부쳐
주세요. 엄마, 고맙습니다.

Exercises

1. Fill in the blanks based on the narration.

(1)   스티브는 _____ 때문에 마크한테 전화했습니다.

(2)   스티브의 _____는 512-6094입니다.

(3)   민지는 _____ 때문에 엄마한테 전화했습니다.

(4)   민지는 _____야 되는데 돈이 없습니다.

(5)   민지 엄마께서 민지한테 오백 불을 _____ 주실 겁니다.

2. Fill in the blanks with appropriate particles (이/가 or 을/를)

(1)   유미는 돈_____ 많아요.

(2)   우진은 어제 백화점에서 돈_____ 많이 썼어요.

(3)   서울에서는 돈_____ 많이 들어요.

(4)   마크는 서점에서 돈_____ 벌어요 ('to earn money').

CULTURE

분주한 지하철 (Busy subway)

지옥철, which literally means the Hell Train, is a sarcastic nickname for the busy subway in Seoul. Millions of people commute to the heart of Seoul by the subway from the areas surrounding the metropolis.

Commuters can spend an hour or so of their morning plowing their way out of the tightly packed crowd in the subway. To make the time more enjoyable, people tend to bring things to amuse themselves. Many people listen to music with their mp3 player or catch up on TV shows on their multi-function cell phone. Some spend time reading from a handheld e-book reader or a traditional paper book. Yet others read a tabloid given out free at the subway station, looking for celebrity gossip to share with their co-workers.

Once the busiest time is over, people get some breathing room. Just when you think that serenity has finally come to the train, however, you will be awakened from the dream by a voice yelling out for help. Mendicants on the subway start working when it is less busy. They usually tell their sad life stories and ask the passengers for help. Some write down the story on a piece of paper, photocopy it, put a copy on each passenger's lap, give them some time to read, and collect the papers later with money. Some people try to sell products—umbrellas, rubber bands, mini flashlights, and many other items. These subway business-people began to appear after the economic crisis in 1997. Although they sell products for a lower price, the quality, as you might expect, is said to be inferior.

USAGE

A. Making telephone calls

Both the caller and the person called say 여보세요 'hello' when the call is made. To confirm that he or she has dialed the right number, the caller usually asks a question—"Is this Mr. Lee's residence?" "Is this Professor Kim's office?" or the like. This kind of question is often in the [~지요?] form as in the following examples:

A:	여보세요.	Hello.
B:	여보세요.	Hello.
A:	거기 [김 교수님 연구실]이지요?	Is this [Professor Kim's office]?
B:	네, 그런데요.	Yes, it is.
A:	[교수님] 좀 부탁합니다.	May I speak to [Professor Kim]?
	(=[교수님] 좀 바꿔 주세요.)	
B:	네, 잠깐만 기다리세요.	Just a minute, please.

[Exercise 1] Practice the preceding dialogue by substituting the following for the expressions in brackets.

(1)   한국 은행 / 김민호 씨

(2)   꽃집 / 홍수미 씨

(3)   서울 약국 / 박철수 씨

(4)   *마이클네 집 / 마이클

      (*마이클네 집 'the house of Michael's family')

More telephone expressions:

지금 없는데요.	He/she is not here now.
(honorific form: 지금 안 계신데요)	
이따가 다시 전화할게요.	I will call again later.
통화 중이에요.	The line is busy.

[Exercise 2] Read the following telephone numbers.

      (1)   431-7890

      (2)   136-0210

      (3)   667-8903

      (4)   445-7021

[Exercise 3] Ask several classmates their telephone numbers, using the following example as a model.

린다:　샌디 씨, 전화 번호가 뭐예요?
샌디:　947의 6981이에요.

[Exercise 4] Ask your teacher's telephone number.
학생:　　선생님 연구실 전화 번호가 어떻게 되세요?
선생님: 932의 5603이에요.

[Exercise 5] Practice speaking with a classmate using the following situations.

      (1)   You call your girlfriend/boyfriend. She/he is not at home and her/his father asks who is calling. Politely leave your name and tell him that you will call later.

      (2)   You call Professor Kim's residence and his wife picks up the phone. She says that Professor Kim is not there.

B. Making an appointment

To make an appointment for some specific purpose, you can indicate that purpose as follows:

[purpose] 때문에 좀 뵙고 싶은데요 / 만나고 싶은데요.

뵙고 싶은데요 is used to refer to someone higher in social status or older than you are. If you and the person you would like to see are peers, 만나고 싶은데요 is used.

지난 번에 본 시험 때문에 좀 뵙고 싶은데요.
스티브 씨, 숙제 때문에 좀 만나고 싶은데요.

To set a time or date, you can use the following expressions:

무슨 요일이 좋아요?   What day is good for you?
몇 시가 좋아요?   What time is good for you?

You can also suggest a time or date as follows:

[date/day/time] 괜찮으세요?/괜찮아요?   Is . . . okay with you?
              어떠세요?/어때요?   How about . . .?
              좋으세요?/좋아요?   Is . . . good for you?
A: 교수님, 숙제 때문에 좀 뵙고 싶은데요.
      내일 연구실에 계실 거예요?
B: 네, 1시부터 있을 거예요.
A: 그럼, 2시 어떠세요?
B: 2시 괜찮아요.
A: 그럼 내일 2시에 뵙겠습니다.

[Exercise] Practice the following situation with a classmate:

Call your professor and ask for a make-up test. Give a reason why you
couldn't take the test. Make an appointment with the professor for a
specific date and time.

C. Describing illness or pain

A: 어디가 아프세요?   Where does it hurt?
B: [Part of the body]이/가 아파요.

머리가 아파요   to have a headache
목이 아파요   to have a sore throat
이가 아파요   to have a toothache
배가 아파요   to have a stomachache
감기 걸렸어요   to have caught a cold
열이 나요   to have a fever
몸이 안 좋아요   not to feel well

[Exercise 1] Practice the following conversation, and then substitute the conditions indicated by the pictures for the underlined part below.

A: 저는 몸('body')이 안 좋아서 파티에 못 가요.

B: 어디가 아프세요?

A: <u>이가 아파요</u>.

B: 많이 아프세요?

A: 이젠 좀 괜찮아요.

(1) (2) (3)

(4) (5)

D. Making a polite request/question

실례지만 'Excuse me but, . . .' or 실례합니다 'Excuse me' is used to show politeness before you ask a question. Typical uses of 실례지만 include asking directions on the street or confirming a telephone number you have just dialed.

Examples

(1) On the street:

> A: 실례지만 말씀 좀 묻겠습니다.
> Excuse me, but may I ask you something?
> B: 네.
> Yes.

(2) On the telephone:

> A: 실례지만 김 교수님 좀 바꿔 주시겠습니까?
> Excuse me, but is Professor Kim there?
> B: 지금 안 계신데요.
> No, he is not here.

(3) Office visit:

> A: 저어, 여기가 김 교수님 연구실입니까?
> Is this Professor Kim's office?
> B: 네. 그런데요. 실례지만 무슨 일로 오셨어요?
> Yes, it is. How can I help you?

[Exercise] Using 실례지만, ask your classmate

(1) how old she or he is.

(2) whether he/she has a boy/girlfriend.

(3) where he/she bought the clothes that she/he is wearing.

(4) what size shoes he/she is wearing.

Lesson 13 - On the Telephone

CONVERSATION 1: May I speak to Steve?

(Soobin calls Steve to find out why he was absent.)

	(ring ring)
Steve:	Hello?
Soobin:	Is this Steve's residence?
Steve:	Yes, it is.
Soobin:	May I speak to Steve, please?
Steve:	Speaking. May I ask who's calling?
Soobin:	It's Soobin Kim. Why weren't you at school today?
Steve:	I couldn't go because I caught a cold.
Soobin:	Is it bad?
Steve:	I was pretty sick in the morning, but I feel better now.
Soobin:	Are you coming to school tomorrow?
Steve:	Yes, I have to go to school for an exam.
Soobin:	Oh, really? Then be sure to get some rest.
Steve:	Yes, I will. Thanks for calling.
Soobin:	Sure, I'll call you again later.

CONVERSATION 2: Is this Professor Park's residence?

(Mark calls Professor Park, and his wife answers the phone.)

	(ring ring)
Mrs. Park:	Hello?
Mark:	Hello? Is this Professor Park's residence?
Mrs. Park:	Yes, it is.
Mark:	May I speak to Professor Park, please?
Mrs. Park:	Yes, hold on one moment. Honey, phone call for you.
Prof. Park:	Hello, this is Park.
Mark:	This is Mark Smith. I was wondering if I could see you to talk about the Korean language class. Are you coming to school tomorrow?
Prof. Park:	Yes, I'll be in my office from two to four in the afternoon.
Mark:	Then I'll go to your office by two-thirty tomorrow.

Prof. Park: All right. See you tomorrow.
Mark: Thank you. Goodbye.

NARRATION: Phone message

1.   (Steve leaves a voice message on Mark's phone.)

Hello Mark! It's Steve Wilson. I'm calling to talk about our Korean language class assignment. I would like to see you ten tomorrow morning in front of the school library. Does that time work for you? Please call me. My number is 512-6094. Bye.

2.   (Minji leaves a voice message on her mom's phone.)

Mom, it's Minji. How have you been? I am doing all right at school. I have to buy some books, but I used all the money I received last month. It costs a lot of money to live in Seoul because of the high living expenses. I'm really sorry, but could you please send some money to my bank account? Five hundred dollars will work. Thanks, Mom.

14과 공항에서   **[At the Airport]**

Conversation 1	토요일이라서 길이 막히네요.

(Mark takes a taxi to Incheon International Airport.)

기사: 어디까지 가세요?

마크: 인천 공항까지 가 주세요.

           오늘은 길이 많이 막히네요.

기사: 토요일이라서^{G14.1} 그래요.

마크: 공항까지 얼마나 걸릴까요?

           30분쯤 걸릴까요?

기사: 글쎄요, 그렇게 빨리 가지는 못 할^{G14.2} 거예요.

           적어도 한 시간은 걸리겠는데요.

마크: 네, 알겠습니다.

           (at the airport)

기사: 손님, 공항 다 왔어요.

마크: 얼마 나왔어요, 기사 아저씨?

기사: 79,000원입니다.

마크: 여기 있습니다. 수고하세요.

기사: 감사합니다.

NEW WORDS

NOUN		ADVERB	
공항	airport	적어도	at least
기사	driver	빨리	fast, quickly
길	street, road	**VERB**	
모레	the day after tomorrow	건너다	to cross
손님	guest, customer	(돈을) 내다	to pay
아저씨	mister; a man of one's parents' age	수고하다	to put forth effort, take trouble
연락	contact	운전하다	to drive
인천	Incheon	**SUFFIX**	
전	before	~(이)라서	because N am/are/is
후	after	~지 못하다	cannot (long form of negation)
휴일	holiday, day off		

NEW EXPRESSIONS

1. 어디까지 가세요? (lit. How far are you going?) is used instead of 어디 가세요? 'Where are you going?' to emphasize the final destination.

2. In 토요일이라서 그래요 (lit. Because it is Saturday, it is like that), the predicate 그래요 refers to the previous statement, 길이 많이 막히네요.

3. 다 왔어요 (lit. Came all the way.) is often used to express that someone has arrived at the destination.

4. 얼마 나왔어요? 'How much did the bill come up?' refers to the fare shown on the taxi meter.

5. 기사 in 기사 아저씨 is a way to address a cab driver. 기사 literally refers to a person trained in engineering, architecture, or the like.

6. 수고하세요 'Thanks for your trouble' can be used to a taxi driver when you get out of the taxi. 수고하셨어요 (lit. You put forth such an effort) can also be used to express appreciation to someone who has just done something for you. These expressions are usually avoided when speaking to a hierarchical superior.

Exercises

1. Fill in the blanks with appropriate words.

      (1)   _____에서 비행기를 타요.

      (2)   택시를 운전하는 사람은 _____예요.

      (3)   돈을 내고 택시를 타는 사람은 _____이에요.

      (4)   내일 다음은 _____예요.

      (5)   _____에는 수업도 없고 일도 안 해요.

2. Fill in the blanks by spelling out the price of each item.

5,700원	25,000원	116,000원	14,000원

      (1)   바지는 _____원이에요.

      (2)   사전은 _____원이에요.

      (3)   커피는 _____원이에요.

      (4)   가방은 _____원이에요.

3. Complete the following dialogue between a customer and a cab driver.

      기사: _____까지 가세요?

      마크: 공항이요. 공항까지 얼마나 _____?

      기사: 글쎄요, _____ (at least two hours)은
                  걸리겠는데요.

      기사: 손님, 다 왔어요.

      마크: _____? (How much is it?)

      기사: 32,000 원입니다.

마크: 여기 있습니다.

_____ (Thank you for your trouble.)

기사: 감사합니다.

GRAMMAR

G14.1   N(이)라서 'because it is N'

Examples

(1)   A: 지난 학기 잘 보냈어요?   How was your semester?

      B: 첫 학기**라서** 좀 바빴어요.   Because it was my first
                                          semester, I was a little busy.

(2)   A: 공항까지 얼마나 걸릴까요?   How long (do you think) will
                                          it take to get to the airport?

      B: 30분 후부터 길이 막히는   Because it is rush hour in 30
           시간**이라서** 오래 걸릴   minutes, I guess it will take
           거예요.   a long time.

Notes

1. The pattern [Clause 1~어서/아서 + Clause 2] is used to explain the cause of the event in clause 2 (G10.4). When ~어서/아서 occurs with [N이다] 'to be', it becomes [N(이)라서]. 이라서 occurs after a noun ending in a consonant, and 라서 occurs after a noun ending in a vowel.

N(이)다	N(이)라서	
학생이다	학생이라서	because someone is/was a student
겨울이다	겨울이라서	because it is/was winter
교수다	교수라서	because someone is/was a professor
의사다	의사라서	because someone is/was a doctor

2. The negative form of [N(이)라서] is [N이/가 아니라서].

학생이 아니라서   교수가 아니라서
의사가 아니라서   겨울이 아니라서

Exercise

Complete the following dialogues, using the form N(이)라서.

(1)   A: 오늘 왜 길에 차가 없어요?

       B: [holiday] 휴일이라서 그래요.

(2)   A: 왜 운전을 안 하세요?

       B: [15 years old] _____ 운전을 아직 못 해요.

(3)   A: 왜 한국어를 배우세요?

       B: 여자 친구가 [Korean]_____ 한국어를
             배워요.

(4)   A: 돈이 많으세요 ?

       B: 아니요. 저는 [student]_____ 돈이
             없어요.

(5)   A: 오늘 날씨가 참 따뜻하지요?

       B: 네, [spring]_____ 따뜻해요.

G14.2 The negative ~지 못하다

Examples

(1)	A:	내일 수영하러 가세요?	Are you going to go swimming tomorrow?
	B:	아니요, 바빠서 주말 전에는 가**지 못할** 거예요.	No, since I'm busy, I won't be able to do that before Saturday.

(2)   그동안 연락 드리**지 못해서**
(= 연락 못 드려서) 정말
죄송합니다.

I am very sorry for not
having been able to contact
you for some time.

(3)   일이 많아서 쉬**지 못하는**
휴일도 있습니다.

There are holidays without
rest for me because I have
lots of work to do.

Notes

[못 + Verb] indicates inability to do something (G6.4). The construction
[verb stem~지 못하다] expresses the same notion in general. Verb stem~지
못하다 is slightly more formal than [못 + Verb].

Exercise

Change the following sentences using ~지 못하다.

(1)   배가 아파서 음식을 못 먹어요.

(2)   시간이 없어서 숙제를 못 했어요.

(3)   감기에 걸려서 일하러 못 갔어요.

(4)   미국에 간 스티브한테서 아직 연락을 못 받았어요.

(5)   모레는 수업이 있어서 파티에 못 갈 거예요.

(6)   돈이 없어서 전화비('phone bill')를 아직 못 냈어요.

(7)   차가 너무 많아서 길을 못 건너겠어요.

Conversation 2   마중 나왔어요.

(Mark runs into Soobin at the airport.)

마크: 어, 수빈 씨, 여기 웬일이세요?

수빈: 마크 씨, 안녕하세요? 큰아버지 마중
          나왔어요.
          마크 씨는 공항에 웬일이세요?

마크: 오늘 영국에서 여동생이 와서 마중 나왔어요.

수빈: 아, 그래요? 몇 시 비행기인데요?

마크: 3시 비행기인데 제가 좀 늦게^{G14.3} 도착했어요.

수빈: 공항까지 뭐 타고 오셨는데요?

마크: 택시 탔어요.

수빈: 택시비 많이 나왔겠네요.
          다음에는 택시를 타지 마세요. ^{G14.4}
          공항 버스가 싸고 편해요.

마크: 아, 몰랐어요.^{G14.5}
          다음에는 공항 버스를 타야겠네요.
          공항 버스는 어디서 타요?

수빈: 출구 바로 앞에 정류장이 있어요.

쪽

NEW WORDS

NOUN		ADJECTIVE	
게임	game	배(가) 부르다	to have a full stomach
계단	stairs	붙러요	
곳	place	적다	to be few, scarce
노래방	karaoke (bar)	말라요	
목소리	voice	VERB	
엘리베이터	elevator	(노래) 부르다	to sing
웬일	what matter	도착하다	to arrive
정류장	(bus) stop	마중 나오다/ 마중 나가다	to come/go out to greet someone
출구	exit		
큰아버지	uncle (father's older brother)	목(이) 마르다	to be thirsty
		졸다	to doze off
택시비	taxi fare		
휴게실	lounge	SUFFIX	
ADVERB		~게	adverbial suffix
더	more	~지 말다 (마세요)	to stop, cease

들어 가는것
나가는 것

출발 /
입구 → 출구

NEW EXPRESSIONS

1. 마중 나오다/나가다 means 'to come/go to a place (e.g., an airport) to greet/meet someone'. 마중 means 'receiving or meeting someone'.

2. 웬일이세요? 'What brings you here?, What are you doing here?' shows surprise when you see an acquaintance unexpectedly.

3. 택시비 'taxi fare' is a combination of the noun 택시 'taxi' and the morpheme 비 'cost', which can be used with other nouns as shown in the following:

전화비	telephone expenses	학비	tuition (fees)
버스비	bus fare	차비	carfare

Exercises

1. Fill in the blanks with appropriate expressions.

상전 – "상중"

(1)   버스는 _____정류장_____에서 타요.

(2)   비행기가 20분 후에 _____ 거예요.

(3)   택시를 타서 _____가 많이 나왔어요.

(4)   _____는 아버지의 형이에요.

(5)   공항에 _____ 나온 사람들이 많았어요.

(6)   _____로 나가세요.

2. Match the most appropriate response from the right column to the question from the left column. Practice the conversation after the match is done.

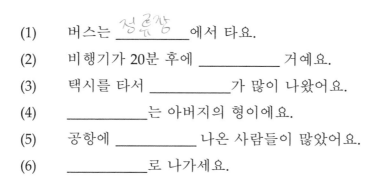

(1)   (우체국에서)
       여기 웬일이세요?   •   • 공항까지
                                     가주세요.

(2)   얼마 나왔어요?   •   바빠서
                                   택시 타고 왔어요.

(3)   공항까지
       택시를 탈까요?   •   • 편지 부치러
                                     왔어요.

(4)   버스를
       어디서 타요?   •   • 이만 칠천 원
                                     나왔습니다.

(5)   (택시 안)
       어디까지 가세요?   •   • 출구로 나가서
                                     길을 건너세요.

(6)   여기까지
       뭐 타고 왔어요?   •   • 택시 타지 마세요.

GRAMMAR

G14.3 The adverbial form ~게

Examples

(1)   A: 오늘 수업에 왜 늦었어요?   Why were you late for class today?

       B: 늦**게** 일어났어요.   I got up late.

(2)   잘 못 들었어요. 크**게** 말해 주세요.   I couldn't hear it. Please
                                           speak loud(ly).

(3)   저녁을 아주 맛있**게** 먹었어요.

(4)   크리스마스를 즐겁**게** 보내세요.

Notes

The adverbial form ~게 refers to the manner or way in which something
happens. ~게 is usually added to an adjective stem.

Adjective	Stem + ~게	Examples
재미있다	재미있게	어제 테니스 게임을 재미있게 봤어요.
바쁘다	바쁘게	지난 주말은 아주 바쁘게 보냈습니다.
시끄럽다	시끄럽게	도서관에서 시끄럽게 얘기하지 마세요.

Exercises

1. Fill in the blanks with an appropriate adverbial form from the box
below.

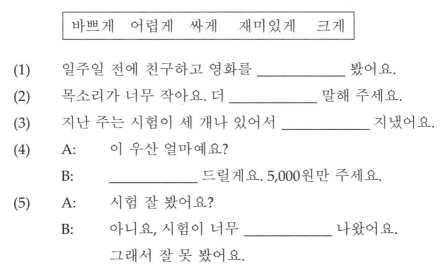

바쁘게   어렵게   싸게   재미있게   크게

(1)   일주일 전에 친구하고 영화를 _____ 봤어요.

(2)   목소리가 너무 작아요. 더 _____ 말해 주세요.

(3)   지난 주는 시험이 세 개나 있어서 _____ 지냈어요.

(4)   A: 이 우산 얼마예요?

       B: _____ 드릴게요. 5,000원만 주세요.

(5)   A: 시험 잘 봤어요?

       B: 아니요, 시험이 너무 _____ 나왔어요.
             그래서 잘 못 봤어요.

G14.4   Negative commands ~지 마세요

Examples

(1)   (Speaker A offers a ride to his friend B, who is coming to visit Korea.)

    A: 제가 공항에 마중 나갈게요.

    B: 복잡한데 나오**지 마세요**.   It's too crowded, so please don't come out to meet me.

(2)   A: 택시를 탈까요?

    B: 택시 타**지 말고** 지하철로 가세요.   Don't take a taxi. Take the subway

instead.

(3)   수업 시간에 졸**지 마세요**.   Don't doze during the class.

(4)   비가 오는데 운전하**지 마세요**.   It is raining; don't drive.

Notes

1. Prohibition is expressed by ~지 마세요, consisting of two components: negation suffix ~지 and the verb 말다 'to stop (doing) something'. 마세요 is the honorific form of the verb 말다, a verb with an irregular ending with /ㄹ/. /ㄹ/ drops before /ㄴ/, /ㅂ/, and /ㅅ/.

2. When you want to express the idea 'Please don't do X, but instead do Y', use the construction [X~지 말고 Y~(으)세요].

    수업 시간에 얘기하지 말고   Please don't talk during
    선생님 말씀을 잘 들으세요.   class, but listen to the teacher.

    커피 마시지 말고 주스 마셔요.   Please don't drink coffee but juice.

Exercises

1. Make up sentences using ~지 마세요.

2. Complete the following sentences using the ~지 말고 form.

(1)   텔레비전을 <u>보지 말고</u> 공부하세요.

(2)   엘리베이터를 _____ 계단으로 내려가세요.

(3)   시험을 내일 _____ 모레 보세요.

(4)   저녁에는 커피를 _____ 주스를 드세요.

(5)   친구를 학교 식당에서 _____ 휴게실에서
       만나세요.

(6)   한국어 수업 시간에는 영어를 _____ 한국어를
       쓰세요.

G14.5   Irregular predicates in 르

Examples

(1)   A: 한인타운에 가고 싶은데
            지하철이 **빨라**요?

      B: 택시가 더 **빠른**데요.   Taxi is faster.

(2)   A: 더 드세요.   Please have some more.
       B: 아니요, 배가 **불러**서   No, I am too full and I
             못 먹겠어요.   can't eat any more.

(3)   A: 뭐 타고 왔어요?   How did you come to
                                                   school?

       B: 길을 잘 **몰라**서   I took a taxi because I didn't
             택시 타고 왔어요.   know the way.

Notes

When an adjective or verb stem ends in 르 and is followed by ~어/아, the
vowel 으 in 르 is deleted and an additional /ㄹ/ is inserted.

부르 + 어요 →   부르+ ㄹ+ 어요   →   불러요
모르 + 아요 →   모르+ ㄹ+ 아요   →   몰라요
빠르 + 아요 →   빠르+ ㄹ+ 아요   →   빨라요

Dictionary form		~어요/아요	~었/았/ 써어요	~어서/아서	~ㅂ니다
(노래) 부르다	to sing, call	불러요	불렀어요	불러서	부릅니다
모르다	to not know	몰라요	몰랐어요	몰라서	모릅니다
빠르다	to be fast	빨라요	빨랐어요	빨라서	빠릅니다

Exercises

1. Use the ~어요/아요 ending in answering the questions.

(1)   시간이 참 빠르지요? _____

(2)   마크가 노래를 참 잘 부르지요? _____

(3)   스티브 씨 일하는 곳 모르지요? _____

(4)   운동해서 목이 마르지요? _____

2. Conjugate each predicate in parentheses according to its context.

    (1)   A: 왜 버스를 안 탔어요?

                B: 택시가 _____ (빠르다) 택시를 탔어요.

    (2)   A: 왜 연락 안 했어요?

                B: 전화 번호를 _____ (모르다) 연락 못 했어요.

    (3)   A: 어디 가세요?

                B: 노래 _____ (부르다) 노래방에 가요.

    (4)   A: 저 분을 잘 아세요?

                B: 아니요, 잘 _____ (모르다).

Narration 민지의 편지

보고 싶은 어머니, 아버지께,

안녕하셨어요? 할머니께서도 건강하시지요?
그동안 연락 드리지 못해서 정말 죄송합니다. 첫 학기라서
바쁘게 지냈어요. 보내 주신 크리스마스 선물과 편지는
잘 받았습니다. 따뜻한 겨울 옷을 보내 주셔서 정말
고맙습니다. 잘 입을게요.
그 곳 밴쿠버 날씨는 어때요? 여기 서울 날씨는 요즘 아주
춥습니다. 언니, 오빠 모두 보고 싶습니다. 제 안부 좀
전해 주세요. 그럼 크리스마스 즐겁게 보내세요.
그리고 새해 복 많이 받으세요.

2013년 12월 19일
서울에서
사랑하는 딸 민지 올림

NEW EXPRESSIONS

1. In 연락 드리지 못해서 죄송합니다 'I am very sorry that I was not able to contact you', 연락 means 'contact'. Together with the verb 드리다, it means 'to contact (a superior)' (lit. to give contact to a superior). Since the recipients of this letter are Minji's parents, she uses the honorific form 드리다 instead of 주다.

2. The particle 과/와, meaning 'with, and', is more formal than the particles 하고 and (이)랑. 과 is used after a consonant, while 와 follows a vowel as in 책과 가방 and 커피와 차.

3. 안부 (좀) 전해 주세요 is an idiomatic expression meaning 'Please give regards to . . .' This expression can be preceded by [person]한테/께 'to a person'. The particle 께 is used for a senior person whereas 한테 can be used for anybody.

> 언니한테 안부 (좀) 전해 주세요.　　Please give my regards to your sister.
>
> 김 선생님께 안부 (좀) 전해 주세요.　　Please give my regards to Professor Kim.

4. 크리스마스 즐겁게 보내세요 means 'Merry Christmas'. The Sino-Korean word 성탄절 can be used instead of 크리스마스, as in 성탄절 즐겁게 보내세요.

5. 새해 복 많이 받으세요 means 'Happy New Year' (lit. Receive lots of blessings in the new year).

6. 사랑하는 딸 means 'beloved daughter'.

7. 올림 means 'presented by' or 'sincerely yours'. 드림 can be used too.

Exercise

Fill in the blanks with appropriate Korean counterparts.

(1)   Please take good care of your health: _____

(2)   Happy New Year: _____

(3)   Please give my regards to: _____

(4)   Merry Christmas: _____

CULTURE

한국의 종교 (Religions in Korea)

South Korea is a country of great religious diversity and a high degree of religious tolerance. According to a nationwide census done in 2005, about twenty-four million people have affiliation to a religious tradition, accounting for nearly half of the entire population. Christianity and Buddhism are the two biggest religions, making up more than 90 percent of the religious population. Other minor religious traditions such as Confucianism, Won Buddhism, shamanism, and Islam are active but have only a few followers according to the census.

The statistics, however, should be interpreted with caution. First, the teachings of Buddhism and Confucianism run deep in the minds of Koreans. It is not surprising considering the long history of Buddhism and Confucianism from ancient times. The two religious traditions function more as an ethical code and spiritual guideline than as a religious doctrine for Koreans. Second, traditional shamanism is widely accepted. Like Buddhism and Confucianism, shamanism in Korea is well mixed in the life of Koreans. For example, you would go to see a fortune-teller to ask when you will get married or when to move to a new place. You might also get a charm from a fortune-teller to bring good luck and fend off bad luck. When you move furniture in your room, you might take the waterways into consideration according to a shamanistic theory.

[handwritten: 우외 전 하세요 / 좌 전 주세요]

USAGE

A. Taking a taxi

Translate the following expressions into Korean:

[handwritten: drop me off / 내 려 주세요]

    (1)   Please take me to the airport.

        [handwritten: 공항까지 가 주세요]

    (2)   How long will it take to get to the airport?

        [handwritten: 여기서 공항에 얼마나 걸려요?]

    (3)   Please turn right in front of the bank.

        [handwritten: 은행앞에 오른쪽 도세요]

    (4)   How much is the fare?

        [handwritten: 택시에 얼마나 나와 어요]

    (5)   (Paying the fare) Here is the money. Thank you.

        [handwritten: 여기 있습니다. 감사합니다]

B. Writing letters and postcards

The standard format of a Korean letter to a respected person consists of the following elements:

    1. Salutation: _____께 (Dear _____)

    2. Greeting: 안녕하세요? or 안녕하십니까?

    3. Main text

    4. Closing: 안녕히 계세요 or 안녕히 계십시오 (계십시오 is a

               deferential form of 계세요.)

    5. Date: in the order year, month, day ____년 ____월 ____일

    6. Sender's name (followed by 올림/드림 'sincerely' or without it).

Example

이민수 선생님께,

선생님 그동안 안녕하셨습니까? 한국어 반 친구들도 다 잘 있습니까?
저는 지난 8월 24일에 서울에 잘 도착했습니다. 요즘 뉴욕의 날씨는
어떻습니까? 여기 서울은 아직 더운 여름 날씨입니다.
저는 학교에서 가까운 곳에 있는 깨끗하고 조용한 아파트로
이사했습니다.
다음 주부터 새 학기가 시작합니다.
거기 한국어 반 친구들한테 안부 전해 주세요.
안녕히 계세요. 다음에 또 연락 드리겠습니다.

2013년 8월 31일
스티브 윌슨 올림

Read Steve's letter and answer the following questions:

(1)   스티브는 언제 서울에 도착했습니까? _8월 24일_____

(2)   서울 날씨는 어떻습니까? _____더 워요____

(3)   스티브는 언제 이 편지를 썼습니까? _2013년 8월 31일_

(4)   스티브 집은 학교에서 멉니까? _아니요, 가까워요____

(5)   이 편지를 받는 사람은 누구입니까? _이민수 선생님___

(6)   언제 새 학기가 시작합니까? ___다음 주 부터___

(7)   스티브가 사는 아파트는 어떻습니까? ___깨끗하고 조용해 학교에서 가까운_

In writing addresses on an envelope in Korean, the ordering is from general to specific: city name, district, street name, house number, the postal code, then the name of the sender or receiver.

서울시 서구 서대신동 3가 51-80 번지
김민지

서울시 성동구 성수 1가 2동 354-214 번지
박철수 귀하*

(*귀하 'Mr./Mrs./Ms.' is exclusively used in addressing a person on an envelope.)

[Exercise 1] Imagine that you are writing a first letter to your pen pal, a college student in Korea. Introduce yourself in the letter.

[Exercise 2] Imagine that your Korean teacher has gone back to Korea. Write a postcard to him or her in Korean.

[Exercise 3] Write a Christmas card in Korean to your classmates.

[Exercise 4] Make a Korean version of the following business card.

Dongho Lee, Professor

Dept. of Korean Language
Korea University
1 Anam-dong Songbuk-gu
23-150　　　Seoul, Korea

[Exercise 5] Complete the following letter written by 유미 to her parents.

보고 싶은 부모님께,

안녕하셨어요? 건강하시지요? 그동안 _연락_ 드리지 못해서 정말 죄송합니다. 첫 학기라서 바쁘게 지냈습니다. 보내 _주신_ 크리스마스 선물은 잘 받았습니다. _예쁜_ 모자를 보내 주셔서 정말 고맙습니다. 잘 _입을게요_.
그 곳 시카고 날씨는 어때요? 여기 서울 날씨는 요즘 아주 춥습니다. 할아버지, 할머니도 보고 싶습니다. 제 _안부_ 좀 전해 주세요. 그럼, 크리스마스 _잘_ 보내세요. 그리고 새해 _받으세요_.

2013년 12월 19일
서울에서
사랑하는 딸 유미 _올림_

Lesson 14 - At the Airport

CONVERSATION 1: The traffic is heavy on Saturdays.
(Mark takes a taxi to Incheon International Airport.)

Driver:	Where are you going?
Mark:	Incheon Airport, please. There's heavy traffic today.
Driver:	Because it's Saturday.
Mark:	How long will it take to the airport? About half an hour?
Driver:	Well, it won't be that fast. It will take at least an hour, I guess.
Mark:	All right.
	(at the airport)
Driver:	This is it. We are at the airport.
Mark:	How much is it?
Driver:	It's 79,000 won.
Mark:	Here it is. Thank you.
Driver:	Thank you.

CONVERSATION 2: I came out to greet somebody.
(Mark runs into Soobin at the airport.)

Mark:	Hey, Soobin. What are you doing here?
Soobin:	Hi, Mark! I came out to greet my uncle. What are you doing here at the airport?
Mark:	My younger sister's arriving from England today.
Soobin:	Oh, really? When is her arrival time?
Mark:	Three o'clock. I came a bit late.
Soobin:	How did you get here?
Mark:	I took a taxi.
Soobin:	The fare must have been a lot. Next time, don't take a taxi. Airport shuttle is cheap and convenient.
Mark:	I didn't know. I should take the shuttle next time. Where does the shuttle stop?
Soobin:	There is a stop right in front of the exit.

NARRATION: Minji's letter

Dear Mom and Dad,

How are you? How is grandma? I'm really sorry I did not write sooner. Since it's my first semester, I've been pretty busy. Thank you for your Christmas card and gift. Thank you so much for the warm winter clothes. I will wear them well.

     How is the weather in Vancouver? The weather in Seoul is very cold these days. I miss everyone back home. Please give them my love. Have a merry Christmas and a happy new year!

December 19, 2013
From Seoul
Love,
Your daughter
Minji

15과 쇼핑 [Shopping]

Conversation 1 | 어서 오세요.

(Mark is shopping at Dongdaemun Market.)

점원: 어서 오세요. 뭐 찾으세요?

마크: 까만색 운동화를 찾는데요.

점원: 네, 이쪽으로 와서 보세요.

마크: 저거 얼마예요?

점원: 44,000 원이에요.

사이즈가 어떻게 되세요?

마크: 270인데요. 여기 양말도 팔아요?

점원: 네, 지금 세일이라서 세 켤레에

만 원에 드릴 수 있어요. G15.1

마크: 그럼 운동화하고 양말 세 켤레 주세요.

점원: 네, 금방 갖다 드릴게요. G15.2

NEW WORDS

NOUN		VERB	
까만색	black (=까망)	갈아 입다	to change (clothes)
사이즈	size	갈아 타다	to change (vehicles)
세일	sale	갖고 가다	to take
양말	socks, stockings	갖고 오다	to bring
운동화	sports shoes, sneakers	갖고 다니다	to carry around
		갖다 놓다	to bring/put down somewhere
점원	clerk, salesperson		
ADVERB		갖다 주다/	to bring/take
금방	soon	드리다*hum.*	something to someone
어서	quick(ly)	걸어가다	to go on foot
		걸어오다	to come on foot
COUNTER		걸어다니다	to walk around
번	number of times (e.g., 한 번, 두 번)	돌아오다	to return, come back
		타고 가다	to go riding
켤레	pair	타고 오다	to come riding
SUFFIX		타고 다니다	to come/go riding
~(으)ㄹ 수 있다/없다	can/cannot	**PARTICLE**	
		에	for, per

NEW EXPRESSIONS

1. 어서 오세요 (lit. Come in quickly) is used to welcome customers or guests.

2. 이쪽 means 'this way, this direction'. 쪽 has two meanings: (a) page, e.g., 책 9쪽을 보세요, and (b) direction or side, e.g., 이쪽으로 오세요 'Come this way please', 오른쪽 'the right side', and 왼쪽 'the left side'.

3. The particle 에 in 세 켤레에 means 'for, per'.

4. Shoe size 270 means 270mm.

Exercise

Complete the following dialogue.

점원: _____. 뭐 찾으세요?
손님: _____ 있어요?
점원: 네, 이 쪽으로 오세요.
　　 여기 많이 있어요.
손님: 이거 _____?
점원: 26,000원입니다.
손님: 저기 저 양말은요?
점원: 한 _____에 2,000원입니다.

GRAMMAR

G15.1 ~(으)ㄹ 수 있다/없다 'can/cannot'

Examples

(1)   A: 지금 운전해 **줄 수 있어요**?
       B: 미안해요. 너무 피곤해서 못 해요.

(2)   A: 내일 만날까요?   Shall we meet tomorrow?
       B: 미안해요.   Sorry. I'm afraid I'm too
             바빠서 **만날 수 없어요**.   busy.

(3)   A: 전화 좀 **쓸 수 있**을까요?   Can I use your phone?
       B: 그러세요 (=그렇게 하세요).
             전화가 방 안에 있어요.

Notes

1. The construction [verb stem~(으)ㄹ 수 있다/없다] 'can/cannot' indicates the possibility or ability of doing something for a given, specific moment.

2. 할 수 없다 is equivalent to 못 하다 and [verb stem~지 못하다].

약속이 있어서 파티에 갈 수 없었어요 (= 가지 못했어요).
컴퓨터가 너무 비싸서 살 수 없었어요 (= 사지 못했어요).

Exercises

1. Answer the following questions:

(1)   한국 노래 부를 수 있어요?

네, 부를 수 있어요.

(2)   인터넷에서 운동화도 살 수 있었어요?

_____

(3)   한국어 숙제가 어려운데 혼자 할 수 있어요?

_____

(4)   김치를 먹을 수 있어요?

_____

(5)   공항에서 택시를 탈 수 있어요?

_____

2. Interview your partner.

(1)   일하고 싶지요? 무슨 일을 할 수 있어요?
(2)   배가 고프지요? 무슨 음식을 만들 수 있어요?
(3)   밖에 비가 오는데 무슨 운동을 할 수 있어요?
(4)   친구들과 노래방에 가요. 어떤 노래를 부를 수 있어요?

G15.2 Compound verbs

Examples

(1)   A: 집에 **걸어 가**세요?
       B: 집이 가까워서 학교에 **걸어 다녀**요.

(2)　　버스가 안 오네요.　　　　　The bus is not coming.
　　　그냥 택시 **타고 갈**까요?　　Shall we just take a taxi?

(3)　　A:　내일 학교에 사전을 **갖고 갈**까요?
　　　B:　네, **갖고 오세**요.

Notes

There are many compound verbs in Korean. 가다, 오다, and 다니다 are
some commonly used verbs that are used together with other verbs. 가다
adds the meaning of "to go" and 오다, "to come," while 다니다 is used for
repeated action.

			가다	오다	다니다
들다	to enter		들어가다	들어오다	-
나다	to exit		나가다	나오다	-
내리다	to descend	~어/아	내려가다	내려오다	-
돌다	to turn		돌아가다	돌아오다	-
오르다	to ascend		올라가다	올라오다	-
걷다	to walk		걸어가다	걸어오다	걸어다니다

방으로 들어가세요.
한국에서 지난 주에 돌아왔어요.

타다	to ride		타고 가다	타고 오다	타고 다니다
입다	to wear	~고	입고 가다	입고 오다	입고 다니다
갖다	to possess		갖고 가다	갖고 오다	갖고 다니다

학교에 걸어오세요, 차 타고 오세요?
가방에 뭐 갖고 다니세요?

			Other verbs
갈다	to change	~어/아	갈아입다
			갈아타다

학교에 오는데 버스를 갈아타세요?
옷을 하루에 몇 번 갈아입으세요?

갖다	to possess	~다	갖다 주다/ 드리다 (humble form)

운동화 좀 갖다 주세요.
할머니께 물 좀 갖다 드리세요.

Exercise

Complete the sentences below with a compound verb from the box. Use
appropriate suffixes for each verb.

들어가다	나가다	돌아가다	걸어다니다
갖다 주다	올라가다	갈아타다	갖다 놓다

(1)   엘리베이터를 타고 1층에서 5층까지 [climb and go]

        _____

(2)   여기 물 좀 [possess and give] _____

(3)   서점을 찾으세요? 저 쪽 건물에서 왼쪽으로

        [turn and go] _____ 그럼 오른쪽에 있습니다.

(4)   눈이 옵니다. 밖에 [exit and go] _____ 싶어요.

(5)   극장 앞에서 76번 버스로 [change and ride] _____

(6)   차가 없어서 집에서 학교까지 [walk regularly] _____

(7)   날씨가 추워서 방으로 [enter and go] _____

(8)   도서관에서 책을 빌려서 선생님 연구실에 [possess and put

        down]_____

Conversation 2   이 서점에 자주 오세요?

(Soobin and Woojin meet at Kyobo Bookstore.)

수빈: 아, 우진 씨. 책 사러 오셨어요?

우진: 네, 친구 졸업 선물을 사러 왔어요.

수빈: 이 서점에는 자주 오세요?

우진: 네, 거리도 제일 가깝고 늦게까지 문을 열어서
        자주 와요. 수빈 씨는요?

수빈: 저도 가끔 와서 커피 마시면서[G15.3] 잡지도
        보고 그래요. 오늘은 별로 할 일이[G15.4] 없어서
        그냥 책 좀 보러 왔어요.

우진: 그래요? 그럼 친구 선물을 아직 못 골랐는데
        커피 마시고 나서[G15.5] 저 좀 도와 줄래요?

수빈: 네, 그럼요.

NEW WORDS

NOUN		VERB	
거리	① distance; ② street	구경하다	to look around; to sightsee
계획(하다)	plan	고르다	to choose, select
등산(하다)	hiking	세수하다	to wash one's face
목욕(하다)	bath	손(을) 씻다	to wash one's hands
문	door	열다	to open
샤워(하다)	shower	이(를) 닦다	to brush one's teeth
잡지	magazine		
졸업(하다)	graduation	**SUFFIX**	
화장실	bathroom, restroom	~고 나서	after
ADVERB		~(으)면서	while ~ing
별로	not really	~(으)ㄹ	noun modifying form (prospective)
제일	first, most		

NEW EXPRESSIONS

1. Here are some useful words and expressions indicating frequency:

가끔	once in a while
자주	often
한 번도 안	not even once, never
얼마나 자주	how often?
매일 (날마다)	every day
하루에 한 번	once a day
하루에 한 번쯤	about once a day
한 달에 두 번	twice a month
일 주일에 한 번쯤	about once a week
일 년에 두 번쯤	about twice a year

2. [N도 V~고 그래요] is used when enumerating several possibilities. The particle 도 is added to a noun(s), and the suffix ~고 is attached to the verb stem(s).

3. 별로 usually occurs with a negative verb or adjective. It means 'not particularly, not really, not so much'.

Exercise

Complete the following sentences using the words in the box below.

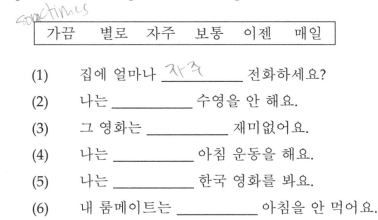

가끔	별로	자주	보통	이젠	매일

sometimes

(1)   집에 얼마나 ___자주___ 전화하세요?

(2)   나는 _____ 수영을 안 해요.

(3)   그 영화는 _____ 재미없어요.

(4)   나는 _____ 아침 운동을 해요.

(5)   나는 _____ 한국 영화를 봐요.

(6)   내 룸메이트는 _____ 아침을 안 먹어요.

GRAMMAR

G15.3   ~(으)면서 'while ~ing'

Examples

(1)   내 친구는 등산하**면서** 보통 음악을 들어요.

(2)   운전하**면서** 전화하지 마세요.

(3)   저는 보통 아침을 먹**으면서** 신문을 읽어요.

(4)   폴은 샤워하**면서** 이를 닦았어요.

Notes

1. ~(으)면서 'while' is used to express two simultaneous actions carried out by the same subject.

2. Note that tense is not marked in the subordinate clause, but is determined by the main clause as in (4).

Exercises

1. What else can you do while you are engaged in the following activity?

(1)   음악을 듣다   음악을 들으면서 책을 읽어요.

(2)   커피를 마시다 _____

(3)   운전하다   _____

(4)   신문을 읽다   _____

(5)   아침을 먹다   _____

(6)   걸어 가다   _____

2. Ask your partner these questions, and tell the class the answers.

(1)   빨래를 하면서 보통 뭐 해요?   _____

(2)   아침을 먹으면서 신문을 읽어요?   _____

(3)   라디오를 들으면서 공부해요?   _____

(4)   영화 보면서 보통 뭐 먹어요?   _____

(5)   버스를 기다리면서 보통 뭐 해요?   _____

G15.4 The noun-modifying form [Verb~(으)ㄹ] + N (prospective)

Examples

(1)   A: 이번 주말에 **할** 일이 많아요?   Do you have lots of things to
                                              do this weekend?

       B: 네, 좀 많아요.   Yes, I do.

(2)   생일 파티에 **입을** 옷이 없어요.   I don't have clothes to wear
                                          to the birthday party.

(3)   다음 학기에 한국어를   The person who will teach
       가르치실 분은 박 선생님이세요.   Korean next semester is
                                          Professor Park.

Notes

The noun-modifying form ~(으)ㄹ indicates that a situation is yet to be realized. In (1) above, 할 일 means 'things to do', in (2) 입을 옷 'clothes to wear', and in (3) 가르치실 분 'the person who will teach'.

Exercises

1. Fill in the blanks with the ~(으)ㄹ form.

    (1)   오늘 저녁에 (먹다)_____먹을_____ 음식이 없어요.

    (2)   내년 여름에 한국에 (가다)_____갈_____ 친구가 많이 있어요.

    (3)   다음 학기에 (졸업하다)_____졸업할_____ 학생이 두 사람 있어요.

    (4)   목이 말라요. (마시다)_____마실_____ 물 좀 주세요.

2. Translate the following sentences into Korean using the ~(으)ㄹ form:

    (1)   This is the present that I will give to my older brother.

    (2)   Professor Kim is the teacher who will teach us from next week on.

    (3)   This is the newspaper that I will read in the lounge.

    (4)   There are lots of things to do this weekend.

G15.5 The clausal connective ~고 나서

Examples

(1) A: 언제 숙제 했어요?   When did you do your homework?

      B: 목욕 **하고 나서** 했어요. I did it after taking a shower.

(2) A: 수업 끝나고 **나서** 뭐 할 거예요?

      B: 백화점에 신발 구경하러 갈 거예요.

(3)　A:　졸업하**고 나서** 뭐 하고 싶어요?
　　B:　아직 계획 못 했어요.

Notes

The construction [verb stem~고 나서] is used when one event or activity has just been finished and another is forthcoming. The event in the main clause occurs after the first action is finished. The ~고 나서 form is attached only to a verb stem, not to an adjective stem. It is more definitive than [verb stem~고] because the first action is actually finished before the second starts. Note that the past tense is not used in the first clause.

Exercises

1. Describe the actions shown in the illustrations in sequence.

　　(1)-(2)　공부하고 나서 점심 먹었어요.
　　(2)-(3)　점심 먹고 나서 ＿＿＿＿＿＿＿＿＿＿
　　(3)-(4)　＿＿＿＿＿＿＿＿＿＿＿＿＿＿＿＿＿
　　(4)-(5)　＿＿＿＿＿＿＿＿＿＿＿＿＿＿＿＿＿
　　(5)-(6)　＿＿＿＿＿＿＿＿＿＿＿＿＿＿＿＿＿

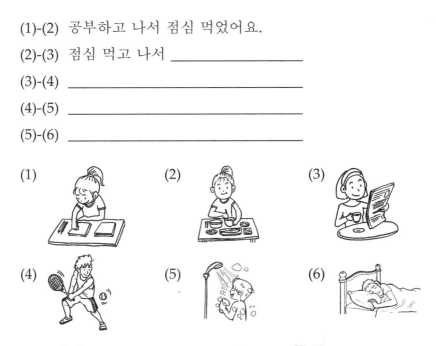

(1)　　(2)　　(3)
(4)　　(5)　　(6)

2. Using ~고 나서, fill in the blanks according to the context.

　　(1)　　스티브는 6시에 저녁을 먹습니다. <u>저녁을 먹고 나서</u>
　　　　　도서관에 가서 공부를 합니다. <u>도서관에서 공부하고 나서</u>
　　　　　집에 10시에 옵니다.

(2)   우진은 9시에 한국어 수업이 있습니다.

_____ 10시에 랩에 가서 한국어 연습을

합니다. _____ 11시 반에 학교 식당에서

친구를 만납니다.

(3)   친구를 만나서 12시에 점심을 먹습니다.

_____ 1시에 테니스를 칩니다.

_____ 3시에 도서관에 가서 공부를 합니다.

_____ 6시쯤 기숙사에 돌아옵니다.

기숙사에 돌아와서 6시 반쯤 저녁을 먹습니다.

(4)   아침에 일어나서 화장실에 가서 손을 씻습니다.

_____ 이를 닦습니다. _____

세수합니다.

3. Fill in the blanks with ~고 나서 and an event that can serve as a time
reference.

(1)   A: 내일 백화점에 몇 시쯤 가실래요?

       B: 수업 <u>끝나고 나서</u> 1시쯤 어때요?

       A: 네, 좋아요.

(2)   A: 저녁에 보통 뭐 해요?

       B: _____

(3)   A: 숙제 때문에 뵙고 싶은데 몇 시쯤 갈까요?

       B: _____ 10시쯤 어때요?

       A: 네, 괜찮습니다.

             그럼 수업 끝나고 10시에 뵙겠습니다.

(4)   A: 한국어 숙제 언제 했어요?

       B: _____

Narration | 동대문 시장

어젯밤에 지하철을 타고 동대문 시장[1]에 갔습니다.
동대문 시장은 옷과 신발 등[2]을 파는 한국에서 제일 큰
시장입니다. 물건[3]이 아주 많고 값[4]도 쌉니다. 그래서
많은 사람들이 동대문 시장에 쇼핑을 하러 갑니다.
그리고 동대문 시장은 24시간 문을 열어서 구경하러
걸어다니는 사람들이 많습니다. 시장에서 물건도 사고
옷과 신발도 구경하고 맛있는 음식을 사 먹기(=사서 먹기)
도 합니다. 저는 까만색 운동화와 양말도 사고 김밥[5]도 사
먹었습니다. 운동화와 양말은 세일이라서 아주 쌌습니다.
김밥도 아주 맛있었습니다. 옷 가게와 신발 가게들이
많아서 구경할 게 정말 많았습니다. 다음 주말에도 셔츠와
바지를 사러 또 가고 싶습니다.

1. 동대문 시장: Dongdaemun Market   2. 등: etc.
3. 물건: merchandise   4. 값: price   5. 김밥: *kimbap*

Exercises

1. List the things you can buy at 동대문 시장.

2. Fill in the blanks based on the narration.

(1)   동대문 시장은 한국에서 _____ 큰 시장입니다.

(2)   동대문 시장에서는 _____과 _____ 등을 팝니다.

(3)   동대문 시장은 _____ 문을 엽니다.

(4)   동대문 시장에서 사람들은 _____ 을 구경하고
       맛있는 _____을 사 먹기도 합니다.

CULTURE

인사동 (Insa-dong)

인사동 is one of the places where visitors to Korea almost always drop by to shop for a souvenir. Located in the center of Seoul, 인사동 is very accessible by public transportation and provides an extensive list of items not readily available anywhere else. From handmade teapots made in traditional Korean style to silken 한복 with dashing colors and patterns, 인사동 symbolizes the traditional Korea as it is known to the world.

Aside from being a center for souvenir shopping, 인사동 also is well known for its many art galleries. In

between visits to souvenir shops, you can enter art galleries scattered about the area and appreciate both traditional and modern Korean arts. If you get thirsty, you can go to cafés serving traditional teas, Korean-style shaved ice, and other tasty treats. You might also find Starbucks at 인사동 interesting because this is the only branch with the sign outside written in Korean.

Adjacent to 인사동 is 삼청동, another area popular for cafés, restaurants, and art galleries. 경복궁 is at the entrance to 인사동, and other Joseon dynasty palaces such as 창덕궁, 창경궁, and 덕수궁 are blocks away. 서울시청, 종묘, 광화문 광장, and 청계천 are other attractions close to 인사동.

USAGE

A. Asking about prices; buying things

얼마예요 is used to ask about prices or fares.

A:	이거 얼마예요?	How much is this?
B:	[price] + 원(₩)/불($)이에요.	It is _____ ₩/$.

[Exercise 1] Prepare some shopping lists and exchange the following question and answer.

Example:		
$185	A: 시계 얼마예요?	
	B: 백 팔십 오불이에요.	

[Exercise 2] Play the roles of customer and salesperson.

A: 이 연필 얼마예요?
B: 일 불 오십 전(cent)이에요.

(1) $ 1.50   (2) $ 0.32   (3) $ 15.60

(4) $ 7.20   (5) $ 19.90   (6) $ 8.00

[Exercise 3] Practice the following dialogue.

A: 이거 어디서 샀어요?

B: '하나 백화점'에서 샀어요.

A: 얼마 줬어요?   'How much did you pay?'

B: _____원/불 줬어요.

Using the model dialogue above, ask about things that belong to your classmates.

B. Expressing frequency

얼마나 자주 . . . 어요?/아요? means 'How often do you . . .?' See how it is used in the exchange below.

A: 부모님께 얼마나 자주 연락하세요?
B: 일주일에 한 번쯤 전화해요.

[Exercise 1] Talk with your partner about how often each person at the table engages in each activity.

A: 스티브는 얼마나 자주 쇼핑해요?
B: 한달에 한 번 쇼핑해요.

편의점

전혀 - never, not at all

Name	Shopping	Dating	Coming to school	Exercising	Writing letters
스티브	once a month	once a month	MTWTh (4 times a week)	every day	once a year
민지	every week	once a week	every day	once a month	twice a year
마크	twice a month	never	MWF	twice a week	once a week

[Exercise 2] Interview your classmates.

(1)   백화점에 쇼핑하러 얼마나 자주 가세요?

(2)   얼마나 자주 머리를 자르세요? (머리를 자르다 'to get a haircut')

(3)   얼마나 자주 외식하세요? (외식하다 'to eat out')

(4)   얼마나 자주 영화 보러 극장에 가세요?

(5)   얼마나 자주 정장을 입으세요? (정장 'formal suit or dress')

[Exercise 3] Answer the following questions in Korean:

(1)   올림픽은 얼마나 자주 있어요? (올림픽 'Olympic')

(2)   미국의 대통령 선거는 몇 년에 한 번 있어요? (대통령 선거 'presidential election')

(3)   월드컵은 얼마나 자주 해요? (월드컵 'World Cup')

(4)   학교 신문은 얼마나 자주 나와요?

(5)   한국어 시험은 얼마나 자주 봐요?

야외 것도

Lesson 15 - Shopping

CONVERSATION 1: Please come in.

(Mark is shopping at Dongdaemun Market.)

Store clerk: Please come in. Are you looking for anything particular?
Mark: I'm looking for black sneakers.
Store clerk: Please come this way.
Mark: How much are those?
Store clerk: They're 44,000 won. What's your size?
Mark: Size 270. Do you sell socks, too?
Store clerk: Yes, they are on sale now—10,000 won for three pairs.
Mark: Then I'll take the shoes and three pairs of socks.
Store clerk: I'll bring them right away.

CONVERSATION 2: Do you come to this bookstore often?

(Soobin and Woojin meet at Kyobo Bookstore.)

Soobin: Oh, Woojin. Are you here to buy some books?
Woojin: Yes, I came to buy a gift for my friend's graduation.
Soobin: Do you come to this bookstore often?
Woojin: Yes, I come here often because it is close and it stays open
            late. How about you, Soobin?
Soobin: I come here sometimes to browse through some magazines
            with a cup of coffee. I had some free time today, so I came
            to look at some books.
Woojin: Really? Then, would you help me choose the gift for my
            friend after the coffee?
Soobin: Sure, let's do that.

NARRATION: Dongdaemun Market

Last night I took the subway to the Dongdaemun Market. The
Dongdaemun Market is the largest market in Korea selling such things as
clothes and shoes. Their prices are usually lower than elsewhere. That's

why many people go there for shopping. Because it is open 24/7, there are many people walking about looking around the market. People buy things, window-shop for clothes and shoes, and eat delicious food at the market. I bought a pair of black sneakers and some socks and had some *kimbap*. The sneakers and socks were on sale so they were quite cheap. The *kimbap* was very tasty. There were so many clothing stores and shoe stores that I spent a long time looking around. I want to go again next weekend to buy a shirt and a pair of pants.

16과 음식점에서 [At a Restaurant]

Conversation 1 냉면 먹어 봤어요?

(Soobin, Soobin's mom, Woojin, and Mark enter a Korean restaurant.)

종업원: 어서 오세요. 몇 분이세요?
우진: 네 명인데요. 자리 있어요?
종업원: 네, 이쪽으로 오세요.

(Everybody sits at the table. The server brings water and menus.)

종업원: 주문하시겠어요?
수빈 어머니: 저는 비빔밥 주세요.
우진: 저는 순두부찌개 먹을게요.
수빈: 전 불고기하고 냉면 먹을래요.
                마크 씨, 냉면 먹어 봤어요?G16.1
마크: 네, 학교 식당에서 한 번 먹어 봤는데
                괜찮았어요. 그런데 저는 찬 음식을
                별로 안 좋아하기G16.2 때문에G16.3
                육개장 먹을래요.

종업원:　　　　네, 알겠습니다. 금방 갖다
　　　　　　　드리겠습니다.

NEW WORDS

NOUN		VERB	
과자	chips, cookies, crackers	물어보다	to inquire
냉면	*naengmyŏn* (cold buckwheat noodles)	싫어하다	to dislike
		주문하다	to order
라면	instant noodles (ramen)		
밥	① cooked rice; ② meal	**ADJECTIVE**	
볼링	bowling	뜨겁다	to be hot
비빔밥	*pibimbap* (rice with vegetables and beef)	시원하다	to be cool, refreshing
순두부찌개	spicy soft tofu stew	싫다	to be undesirable
육개장	spicy beef and leek soup	차다	to be cold
음식점	restaurant (=식당)	**SUFFIX**	
자리	seat	~기	nominalizer
종업원	employee	~기 때문에	because
케이크	cake	~어/아 보다	to try to

NEW EXPRESSIONS

1. In 이쪽, 그쪽, and 저쪽, 쪽 indicates direction. 으로 'to, toward' is attached to 쪽, as in 이쪽으로, 그쪽으로, and 저쪽으로, which are synonymous with 이리(로), 그리(로), and 저리(로).

2. Both 주문하다 and 시키다 mean 'to order'. While 주문하다 can refer to any kind of ordering, 시키다 is restricted to ordering in a restaurant.

Exercises

1. Fill in the blanks with appropriate words.

    (1)　　음식을 사서 먹는 곳: 　　식당
    (2)　　식당에서 주문을 받는 사람: 　종업원
    (3)　　식당에서 주문을 하는 사람: 　손님
    (4)　　식당 테이블('table')하고 의자: 　자리

2. List the names of the Korean foods you know.

GRAMMAR

G16.1	~어/아 보다 'try doing'

Examples

(1) A: 비빔밥 **먹어 봤**어요?   Have you eaten *pibimpap*?
     B: 아니요, 안 **먹어 봤**어요.   No, I have not.

(2) A: 이 과자 한번 **드셔 보**세요.   Please try this cracker.
     B: 감사합니다. 아주 맛있어요.   Thank you. It is very
                                        delicious.

(3) A: 밖에 친구가 왔어요.   Your friend is outside.
         나가 보세요.   Please (lit. try) go out and see
                                        him.

Notes

1. The first example above literally means "Did you eat *pibimpap* and see what it was like?" It is different from 비빔밥 먹었어요? 'Did you eat *pibimpap*?' which is a factual question. When ~어/아 보다 is used, it indicates an experience ('have done') or an attempt ('try') as shown below.

한국에 한번 **가 보**세요.   Please try going to Korea.

2. With the meaning of "attempt" or "trial," ~어/아 보다 can be used to express suggestion in the form of ~어/아 보세요.

이 책 재미있어요. 읽어 보세요.
오후에 텔레비전 보지 말고 운동해 보세요.
다음에는 한국 노래를 들어 보세요.

3. Adding 보다 to a verb sometimes creates a new compound verb. For example, 알다 + 보다 = 알아보다 'to inquire into, recognize', and 묻다 + 보다 = 물어보다 'to inquire, ask'.

> A: 학교 전화 번호를 모르는데 누구한테 물어보지요?
> B: 114*에 전화해서 알아보세요.
> (*in Korea, people dial 114 for directory assistance)

There is an idiomatic expression 그만 가 보겠습니다 'Let me excuse myself' (lit. With that much, I will try leaving). In this expression, 보다 adds a nuance of politeness.

Exercises

1. Answer the following questions.

> (1) 도서관에서 일해 봤어요? _____
>
> (2) 정치학 수업을 들어 봤어요? _____
>
> (3) 라면 먹어 봤어요? _____
>
> (4) 서울에 가 봤어요? _____
>
> (5) 테니스 쳐 봤어요? _____

2. Ask your partner whether he or she has had the following experiences, and then switch roles.

> (1) 볼링 치다   Q: 볼링 쳐 봤어요?
>   A: 작년에 한 번 쳐 봤어요.
>
> (2) 호주를 여행하다
>
> (3) 한국 신문을 읽다
>
> (4) 뉴욕에서 택시를 타다
>
> (5) 한국 음식점에 가다
>
> (6) 갈비를 먹다

3. Suggest the following food to your partner:

(1)   육개장   A: 육개장 <u>드셔 보세요</u>.
                              B: 네, 감사합니다.

(2)   따뜻한 커피 한 잔

(3)   시원한 냉면

(4)   뜨거운 라면

(5)   생일 케이크

G16.2 | The nominalizer ~기

Examples

(1)   한국어 수업 시간에 말하**기**,   In Korean class, we learn
       듣**기**, 읽**기**, 쓰**기**를 배웁니다.   speaking, listening, reading,
                                    and writing.

(2)   A: 한국어가 어려워요?
       B: 한글은 쓰**기**는 쉬운데 말하**기**는 어려워요.

(3)   A: 바빠서 아침에 운동하**기**가 힘들어요.
       B: 그럼, 저녁에 해 보세요.

(4)   A: 방학이 벌써 끝났네요.
       B: 공부하**기** 싫어요. 더 놀고 싶어요.

Notes

The nominalizer ~기 is used to form a noun out of a verb, as in
the English gerund. Sometimes ~는 것 (G17.1) and ~기 are used
interchangeably, as in:

       수업 시간에 말하**기**를 배워요.   (We) learn speaking in class.
       수업 시간에 말하**는 것**을 배워요.   (We) learn how to speak in
                                    class.

Exercises

1. Use ~기 to describe what each person below enjoys doing.

(1)   마이클은 주말에 등산을 해요.
       마이클은 주말에 등산**하기를** 좋아해요.

(2)   제니는 영화를 봐요.

_____

(3)   리사는 예쁜 선물을 받아요.

_____

(4)   우진은 방학에 여행을 가요.

_____

(5)   수빈은 어머니하고 전화해요.

_____

(6)   스티브는 음악을 들어요.

_____

2. Make a list of things to do, using the nominalizer ~기.

취미 – hobby

Example:	오늘 저녁	6시에 기숙사 식당에서 밥 먹기
		8시에 학교 커피숍에서 친구 만나기
		8시 반부터 10시까지 영화 보기

(1)   이번 주말
      a.   숙제 하기
      b.
      c.
      d.

(2)   친구 생일 파티 준비하기
      a.   카드 쓰기
      b.
      c.
      d.

| G16.3 | The clausal connective ~기 때문에 (reason) |

Examples

(1)   돈이 없**기 때문에** 책을 못 사요.   Because I don't have
                                            money, I can't buy books.

(2)   이번 주는 시험이 있**기 때문에**
       일을 못 해요.

(3)   A: 왜 오늘 아침에 수업에
             늦었어요?
       B: 밤에 늦게 잤**기 때문에**
             일찍 못 일어났어요.

Notes

1. ~기 때문에 'Because . . .' gives a reason, unlike ~어/아서 (G10.4), which refers to a cause or a developmental sequence. While 때문에 is preceded by a noun (G13.4), the nominalizer ~기 in ~기 때문에 is used with a verb or an adjective.

    수업 때문에 = 수업이 있기 때문에

2. ~기 때문에 differs from ~어서/아서 in some respects:

    (a) ~기 때문에 is used with a tense marker, while ~어서/아서 cannot take any tense marker.

        머리가 아파서 타이레놀을 먹었어요.
        머리가 아팠기 때문에 타이레놀을 먹었어요.

    (b) When you make an excuse, an apology, or an expression of gratitude, it is more appropriate to use ~어서/아서, which implies a situation beyond your control and thus inevitable.

        늦어서 미안합니다.   (not 늦었기 때문에 미안합니다.)
        와 주서서 감사합니다. (not 와 주셨기 때문에 감사합니다.)

Exercises

1. Change the first clause using ~기 때문에. Use the past-tense form if necessary.

    (1)   수지는 아침을 (안 먹다)_____ 점심을 일찍 먹어요.

    (2)   저는 매일 (운동하다) _____ 건강합니다.

    (3)   민지가 점심을 (사다) _____ 우진이가 커피를 샀습니다.

    (4)   토요일 오후에는 교통이 (복잡하다) _____ 지하철을 타요.

    (5)   찬 음식을 (싫어하다) _____ 냉면을 자주 먹지 않아요.

2. Give a reason in response to the following questions using ~기 때문에.

    (1)   A: 왜 피곤해요?

              B: _____

    (2)   A: 왜 육개장을 안 먹어요?

              B: _____

    (3)   A: 왜 어제 산 텔레비전을 다시 가게에 갖다 주었어요?

              B: _____

    (4)   A: 왜 한국어를 배우고 있어요?

              B: _____

    (5)   A: 오늘 왜 수업에 늦었어요?

              B: _____

3. Ask your partner the following questions. Answers should include ~기 때문에, ~어요/아요, ~(으)ㄹ 거예요, or ~어야/아야 돼요.

(1)   A: 학교에 몇 시에 가세요?

      B: 한국어 수업이 있기 때문에 9시까지 가야 돼요.

(2)   A: 주말에 어디 갈 거예요?

      B: _____

(3)   A: 이번 방학에 뭐 할 거예요?

      B: _____

(4)   A: 오늘 몇 시에 점심 먹을 거예요?

      B: _____

(5)   A: 오늘 도서관에서 공부할 거예요?

      B: _____

(6)   A: 오늘 저녁 어디서 먹을 거예요?

      B: _____

Conversation 2 | 육개장이 맵지 않아요?

(The server brings food.)

종업원: 여기 음식 나왔습니다.
               비빔밥 어느 분이세요?

수빈: 어머니 앞에 놓아 주세요.

종업원: 냉면 잘라 드릴까요?^{G16.4}

수빈: 네, 잘라 주세요.

마크, 우진: 잘 먹겠습니다, 어머니.

수빈 어머니: 육개장이 너무 맵지 않아요?^{G16.5}

마크: 괜찮습니다. 아주 맛있어요.
               우진 씨, 순두부찌개는 어때요?

우진: 별로 짜지 않고 맛있네요.

수빈 어머니: (종업원에게) 저어, 여기요!
               김치하고 반찬 좀 더 주세요.

종업원: 네.

(after a while)

마크, 우진: 정말 잘 먹었습니다.

수빈 어머니: 여기요! 계산서 좀 갖다 주시겠어요?

종업원: 네, 알겠습니다.

NEW WORDS

NOUN		VERB	
값	price	놓아 주다/드리다*hon.*	to put something down (for someone)
계산서	check		
김치	*kimchi*	돌려 주다/드리다*hon.*	to return (something to someone)
녹차	green tea		
된장찌개	soybean-paste stew	시키다	to order (food)
메뉴	menu	식사하다	to have a meal
반찬	side dishes	잘라 주다/드리다*hon.*	to cut (something for someone)
샌드위치	sandwich		
식사	meal	ADJECTIVE	
음료수	beverage	달다	to be sweet
피자	pizza	맵다	to be spicy
SUFFIX		않다	to not be, to not do
~어/아	do something for another's benefit	짜다	to be salty
드리다 *hon.*			

NEW EXPRESSIONS

1. Flavors and tastes:

맛	flavor, taste	맛이 있다	to be tasty
		맛이 없다	not to taste good
달다	to taste sweet	쓰다	to taste bitter
싱겁다	to taste bland	짜다	to taste salty
맵다	to taste spicy	시다	to taste sour

2. People also attract a server's attention by calling out 여기요! (lit. Here!).

3. 잘 먹겠습니다 or 맛있게 먹겠습니다 is used as a polite acknowledgment before eating to thank the host, and 잘 먹었습니다 or 맛있게 먹었습니다 after you eat.

4. Parents of your friends are often addressed as 아버님 (honorific form of 아버지) and 어머님 (honorific form of 어머니) as in 잘 먹겠습니다, 어머니.

Exercises

1. Practice ordering food at a Korean restaurant.

```
┌─────────────────────────────┐
│            메뉴              │
│                             │
│  갈비          ₩12,000      │
│  불고기        ₩10,000      │
│  비빔밥        ₩ 5,000      │
│  냉면          ₩ 6,000      │
│  육개장        ₩ 8,000      │
│  순두부찌개    ₩ 5,000      │
│                             │
└─────────────────────────────┘
```

종업원: 어서 오세요. 몇 분이세요?

손 님: _____. 자리가 있어요?

종업원: 네, 이쪽으로 오세요.

　　　　　주문하시겠어요?

손님: _____하고 _____주세요.

손님: 여기요! _____ 더 주세요.

종업원: 네, 알겠습니다.

2. Ask your classmates what foods they like and dislike.

이름	좋아하는 음식	싫어하는 음식

GRAMMAR

| G16.4 | Giving and offering: ~어/아 드리다 |

Examples

(1)   어머니가 뜨거운 음식을 싫어하세요.
       그래서 냉면을 **시켜 드렸어**요.

I ordered *naengmyŏn*
for my mom.

(2)   A: 할아버지 생신에 뭘 **해 드렸**어요?
       B: 식당에서 저녁을 **사 드렸**어요.

(3)   A: 책 좀 **빌려 주**세요.
       B: 네, **빌려 드릴**게요.
       A: 언제까지 **돌려 드릴**까요?
       B: 모레까지 **돌려 주**세요.

Notes

1. The difference between 주다 and 드리다 is illustrated in the picture
below. The plain form 주다 is used to a person of lower status whereas
its humble form 드리다 is used to a senior person or one of higher status
(G9.3).

아버지께서 저한테 가방을 사 주셨어요.

제가 아버지께 가방을 사 드렸어요.

소피아가 저한테 가방을 사 주었어요.

2. The different forms of ~어/아 주다 are as follows:

Plain ~어/아 주다	유진이가 커피를 사 주었습니다.
Subject honorific ~어/아 주시다	선생님께서 저한테 점심을 사 주셨습니다.
Subject humble (recipient honorific) ~어/아 드리다	나는 어머니께 꽃을 사 드렸습니다.
Subject honorific and humble ~어/아 드리시다	어머니께서 할머니께 옷을 사 드리셨습니다.

Exercises

1. Complete the dialogues, using the proper forms of 주다 or 드리다.

    (1)   종업원: 음료수는 뭐 드릴까요?

           손님: 녹차 _____

    (2)   학생: 뭐 시켜 드릴까요?

           선생님: 된장찌개를 _____

    (3)   선생님: 어제 할머니께 책을 읽어 드렸어요?

           학생: 네, 읽어 _____

2. Complete the sentences with one of the verbs of giving in the box below. Use an appropriate suffix for each verb.

주다   주시다   드리다   드리시다

    (1)   어머니가 저한테 돈을 _____

    (2)   내가 친구한테 샌드위치를 만들어 _____

    (3)   저기요, 할머니께 물 좀 갖다 _____

    (4)   선생님께서 아버지께 편지를 보내 _____

3. Answer the following questions using 주다.

(1)   계산서 드릴까요?

네, _____

(2)   볼펜 좀 빌려 주시겠어요?

_____

(3)   냉면은 나중에 시킬까요?

_____

(4)   메뉴 갖다 드릴까요?

_____

G16.5 Negation: ~지 않다

Examples

Statements:

(1)   a. 날씨가 **안** 좋아요.
b. 날씨가 좋**지 않**아요.

(2)   작년에는 한국말을 배우**지 않**았습니다.
시간이 별로 없어서 한국어 수업을 듣**지 않**습니다.

Questions:

(3)   A: 주스가 너무 달**지 않**아요?   Isn't the juice too sweet?
B: 네, 좀 달아요.

(4)   A: 어젯밤에 극장에 사람이
많**지 않**았어요?
B: 네, 정말 많았어요.

Notes

1. In general, the long form of the negative [~지 않다] and the short form [안 + Verb or Adjective] are used interchangeably, although the long form sounds slightly more formal. The long form is much more frequently used in writing than is the short form.

2. ~지 못하다 'cannot' (G14.2) is used instead of ~지 않다 when a situation or external circumstances do not allow a person to do something as in (2).

3. The long form of the negative is used in conversation when the speaker seeks confirmation or agreement from the listener. Stating a belief or an opinion as a negative question is more cautious and more polite as in (4).

Exercises

1. Change the following sentences by using the form ~지 않다.

(1)   오늘은 별로 안 바빠요.

         오늘은 별로 바쁘지 않아요.

(2)   종업원이 계산서를 빨리 안 갖다 줬어요.

         _____

(3)   내일 백화점에 같이 안 갈래요?

         _____

(4)   오늘은 피자를 안 먹고 싶어요.

         _____

(5)   친구가 돈을 안 빌려 줬어요.

         _____

(6)   이 식당은 음식 값이 별로 안 싸요.

         _____

2. Give an appropriate response using the form ~지 않아요?

(1)   밖이 춥습니다. 룸메이트가 짧은 바지를 입고 나갑니다.

   춥지 않아요?

(2)   더운 여름날 아버지가 뜨거운 차를 드십니다.

   _____

(3)   스티브 씨가 매운 김치를 먹습니다.

   _____

(4)   아직 식사를 못 했습니다.

   _____

(5)   언니가 밤에 안 자고 공부합니다.

   _____

Narration | 점심 식사

오늘 우진이[1]와 민지는 학교 앞 '우리식당'에서 점심을
먹었습니다. 학교 앞에는 음식점들이 여러 군데 있는데,
값도 싸고 종업원들도 친절하기 때문에 '우리식당'에
자주 갑니다. 우진이는 비빔밥을, 민지는 된장찌개를
시켰습니다. 비빔밥에 고추장[2]이 같이 나왔는데 우진이는
매운 음식을 싫어하기 때문에 고추장은 넣지[3] 않았습니다.
점심은 전부[4] 12,000원이었습니다. 식사 후에 민지가 점심
값을 냈습니다. 그리고, 커피숍에 가서 우진이는 녹차를
마시고 민지는 커피를 마셨습니다. 이번에는 우진이가
돈을 냈습니다.

1. 이: a suffix inserted after a Korean first name that ends in a consonant
2. 고추장: red-pepper paste
3. 넣다: put in
4. 전부: all together, in total

Exercise

Fill in the blanks based on the narration.

(1)   '우리식당'은 종업원도 _____고 _____도 쌉니다.

(2)   점심에 민지는 _____을 먹고 우진이는 _____를   먹었습니다.

(3)   우진은 _____을 싫어하기 때문에 고추장은 넣지 않았습니다.

(4)   점심은 전부 _____원이었습니다.

(5)   커피숍에서 차를 마시고 우진이가 돈을 _____.

CULTURE

음식 문화 (Food culture)

The importance of rice in the Korean diet cannot be overemphasized. In fact, various terms are used to differentiate rice in different stages: rice seedlings are called 모, rice plants growing in a paddy are called 벼, processed rice without coating is called 쌀, and cooked rice ready to be served is called 밥. Considering the centrality of rice in the Korean diet, it is no coincidence that 밥 refers to an entire meal as well.

A typical Korean meal would start with a bowl of rice and a bowl of soup in front of you. The rice is placed on the left and the soup on the right. Next to the soup are a pair of chopsticks and a spoon. In the common area of the table is food to share. Koreans share food with others at the same table and don't usually mind eating directly from the shared dishes. It is thought to be impolite to make loud sounds when you eat, and you are encouraged not to hold up your bowl of rice with your hands.

Even though 불고기 and 김치 might be the best-known Korean dishes to the world, the single most popular food for eating out in Korea is 삼겹살. It is the part of the pig that comes from the belly and has layers of fat on one end. The most popular way to eat it is to wrap the roast 삼겹살 in a piece of lettuce with such vegetables as garlic, green onion, and chili, and add a special sauce before you pop it into your mouth. 소주 is a popular liquor Koreans enjoy with 삼겹살.

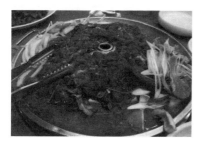

불고기

김치

USAGE

A. Making suggestions

(1)	종업원:	주문하시겠어요?
	손님:	잠깐만요. 메뉴 좀 볼게요.
(2)	종업원:	냉면 잘라 드릴까요?
	손님:	네, 잘라 주세요.
(3)	우진:	점심 뭐 먹을까요?
	마크:	오늘은 피자가 먹고 싶은데요.
	우진:	그럼, 학교 앞 피자 가게로 갈까요?

Several verbal endings may be used in making suggestions or proposals (e.g., ~(으)ㄹ까요? ~어/아 드릴까요? or ~시겠어요?). The choice depends on the formality of the situation and the relationship between the speaker and the listener.

Typically the response to a suggestion is in request form with 주세요. 해 드릴까요? implies that the listener benefits from the action, and 할까요 often involves both parties doing something together.

[Exercise 1] Answer the following suggestions:

(1)   불고기 드릴까요? _____

(2)   문 좀 열까요? _____

(3)   차 한 잔 사 드릴까요? _____

(4)   오늘은 댁에 일찍 들어가시겠어요? _____

(5)   비가 오는데 집에 있을까요? _____

[Exercise 2] Place an order in the restaurants named below.

(1) 한국 음식점   (2) 피자 가게   (3) 커피숍

B. Ordering food

(1)   종업원: 주문하시겠어요?
       손님: 불고기 일 인 분('one portion') 주세요.
       종업원: 네, 알겠습니다. 잠깐만 기다리세요

(2)   종업원: 여기 메뉴 있습니다.
       손님: 스파게티 ('spaghetti')주세요.
       종업원: 마실 거는 뭘 드릴까요?
       손님: 콜라 ('cola')주세요.

(3)   종업원: 뭐 드시겠어요?
       손님: 녹차 있어요?
       종업원: 녹차는 없는데요.
       손님: 그럼, 커피 주세요.

The waiter or waitress in a restaurant usually asks:

주문하시겠어요?   지금 시키실래요?
뭐 드시겠어요?   반찬 더 갖다 드릴까요?

[Exercise 1] Interview your partner; report the answers to the class.

(1)   어떤 음식을 좋아하세요? _____

(2)   보통 무슨 음료수를 마셔요? _____

(3)   어제 저녁에 뭐 먹었어요?_____

(4)   요리하는 것을 좋아하세요? (요리하다 'to cook')

       _____

(5)   어느 식당에 자주 가세요? _____

(6)   보통 어디에서 친구를 만나요? _____

(7)   한국 음식을 좋아하세요? _____

(8)   보통 어디서 점심을 먹어요? _____

(9)   학교 근처에 맛있는 식당이 어디예요? _____

(10)   어디 커피가 맛있어요? _____

[Exercise 2] Here is information about two restaurants in Seoul.
Role-play with your classmate on the following topics:

(1)   삼원 가든
       주소: 서울시 강남구 신사동 623-1
       전화 번호: (02) 548-3030, 544-5351
       지하철 3호선 압구정역에서 택시로 15분

       메뉴
       갈비구이   ₩ 10,000   불고기   ₩ 14,000
       국수전골   ₩ 9,000   비빔밥   ₩ 8,000
       갈비탕   ₩ 9,000   된장 찌개   ₩ 8,000

예약 하고 싶은데요

(2)   우래옥
       주소: 서울 중구 무교동 118-1
       전화 번호: (02) 265-0151/2
       지하철 2호선 을지로 4가역에서 걸어서 3분

       메뉴
       물냉면   ₩ 8,000   비빔 냉면   ₩   8,000
       회 냉면   ₩ 9,000   육회   ₩ 20,000
       된장 찌개   ₩ 4,000   만두국   ₩   7,000

(1)   Call the restaurants and ask for their addresses, phone
       numbers, and directions.

(2)   Call the restaurant and make a reservation for a group of
       20 people. Then ask what's on the menu and order for the
       group.

(3)   You're at the restaurant. Place an order with the waiter/
       waitress.

가능해요?
is it
possible?

C. Describing tastes

[Exercise] Give at least two examples for each category.

(1)   단 음식: _____

(2)   짠 음식: _____

(3)   매운 음식: _____

(4)   찬 음식: _____

(5)   뜨거운 음식: _____

(6)   달고 매운 음식: _____

Lesson 16 - At a Restaurant

CONVERSATION 1: Have you ever tried *naengmyŏn?*
(Soobin, Soobin's mom, Woojin, and Mark enter a Korean restaurant.)

Server:	Welcome. How many people do you have?
Woojin:	Four. Do you have a table?
Server:	Yes, we do. Please follow me.

(Everybody sits at the table. The server brings water and menus.)

Server:	Are you ready to order?
Soobin's mother:	I would like *pibimpap*.
Woojin:	I would like to have soft tofu stew.
Soobin:	I'll get *pulgogi* and *naengmyŏn*. Mark, have you ever tried *naengmyŏn*?
Mark:	Yes, I tried it once at the school cafeteria and it was okay. I am going to try *yukkaejang* this time, though. I don't really like food served cold.
Server:	All right. I will get your food right away.

CONVERSATION 2: Isn't the *yukkaejang* **spicy?**
(The server brings the food.)

Server:	Here you go. Who ordered *pibimpap*?
Soobin:	Please put that in front of my mother.
Server:	Should I cut the *naengmyŏn* noodles?
Soobin:	Yes, please.
Mark, Woojin:	Thank you for the food, mom.
Soobin's mother:	Isn't the *yukkaejang* too spicy?
Mark:	No, it's fine. Very delicious. Woojin, how's the soft tofu stew?
Woojin:	It's delicious, too. It's not too salty.
Soobin's mother:	(to the server) Excuse me, can you get us some more *kimchi* and other side dishes, please?

Server:	Sure.
	(after a while)
Mark, Woojin:	Oh, we are full. Thank you for the food.
Soobin's mother:	Excuse me. Can we get the check, please.
Server:	Sure.

NARRATION: Lunch

Minji and Woojin had lunch at Woori Restaurant in front of the school today. They go there more often than the other many restaurants in front of the school because it costs less and the people there are nicer. Woojin ordered *pibimpap* and Minji got *dwenjang jjigae*. Because Woojin doesn't like spicy food, he didn't add *koch'ujang* to his dish. The lunch was 12,000 won overall. When they were done eating, Minji paid at the counter. Then they went to a café, where Woojin had a green tea and Minji had a coffee. This time, Woojin picked up the check.

17과 취미   [Hobbies]

Conversation 1   취미가 뭐예요?

(Mark and Minji meet at a party.)

마크: 민지 씨, 취미가 뭐예요?

민지: 저는 그림 그리는 걸^{G17.1} 좋아해요. 마크 씨는요?

마크: 저는 음악을 좋아해요.

민지: 무슨 음악을 좋아하세요?

마크: 클래식을 자주 듣는데 그 중에서 바이올린 음악을
제일 좋아해요. 바이올린 연주를 들으면^{G17.2}
기분이 좋아요. 그래서 매일 밤 잠 자기 전에
바이올린 음악을 들어요.
민지 씨도 음악 좋아하세요?

민지: 저는 클래식보다^{G17.3} 록이나 재즈를 많이 들어요.

마크: 록 음악은 좀 시끄럽지 않아요?

민지: 네, 좀 그렇지요. 제가 음악을 크게 틀면
룸메이트가 아주 싫어해요. 그래서 지난 주에
새로 헤드폰을 샀어요.

NEW WORDS

NOUN		VERB	
그림	picture, painting	그리다	to draw
기분	feeling	틀다	to turn on, switch on, play (music)
답	answer		
록	rock music	**ADJECTIVE**	
바이올린	violin	더럽다	to be dirty
서비스	service	편리하다	to be convenient
연주(하다)	musical performance	**ADVERB**	
잠	sleep	가장	the most
재즈	jazz	덜	less
취미	hobby	새로	newly
클래식	classical music	중에서	between, among
헤드폰	headphones		
PARTICLE		**SUFFIX**	
보다	than	~(으)면	if
(이)나	or (with nouns)	~는 것	(an act of) ~ing

NEW EXPRESSIONS

1. A noun can be formed by adding ~(으)ㅁ to a verb stem (ㅁ after a stem ending in a vowel and 음 after a stem ending in a consonant). Stems that end in /ㄹ/ are unpredictable.

그리다	to draw	그림	a painting, a picture
자다	to sleep	잠	sleep
추다	to dance	춤	a dance
꾸다	to dream	꿈	a dream
얼다	to freeze	얼음	ice

Verbs such as 그리다, 추다, and 꾸다 must have an object. Examples:

그림을 그리다	to paint a painting
춤을 추다	to dance a dance
꿈을 꾸다	to dream a dream
잠을 자다	to sleep

2. The following verbs are used for specific musical instruments:

치다	to hit	기타를 치다	play the guitar
		피아노를 치다	play the piano
		드럼을 치다	play the drum
켜다	to play	바이올린을 켜다	play the violin
		첼로를 켜다	play the cello
불다	to blow	클라리넷을 불다	play the clarinet
		플룻을 불다	play the flute

3. The construction [verb stem~기 전에] is used when the event in the second clause occurs before the one in the first clause. The past tense is never expressed in the first clause. Examples:

밥을 먹기 전에 손을 씻어요.	I wash my hands before eating.
미국에 오기 전에 한국대학에서 공부했어요.	I studied at Hankook University before coming to the States.

A noun can precede 전에.

졸업 전에	졸업하기 전에
점심 전에	점심을 먹기 전에
시험 전에	시험을 보기 전에

4. The particle ~(이)나 means 'or' in the following context:

A: 뭐 마실래요?
B: 커피나 차 주세요.

It can also mean 'as much/many as' (G11.3) as in the following example:

이번 학기에 다섯 과목이나 들었어요.

5. 새로 is an adverb form, and 새 is a pre-noun meaning 'new'. Note the differences in the examples below.

새 신발을 샀어요.	I bought a new pair of shoes.
새로 이사 온 학생이 한 명 있어요.	We have a student who recently moved in.
컴퓨터를 새로 샀어요.	I bought a new computer.

Exercises

1. Fill in the blanks with the appropriate verbs.

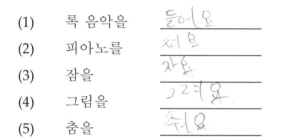

(1)   록 음악을   _들어요_____

(2)   피아노를   _쳐요_____

(3)   잠을   _자요_____

(4)   그림을   _그려요_____

(5)   춤을   _춰요_____

2. Find out the classmates who do the following activities:

(1)   Play the piano/violin/flute/guitar

(2)   Play tennis/baseball/basketball/soccer

(3)   Like classical music/K-pop/rock/jazz

(4)   Like to paint/sleep/listen to loud music

3. Make up a dialogue with your partner.

(1)   Q: (아침 먹다) 아침 먹기 전에 보통 무엇을 해요?

A: 아침 먹기 전에 신문을 봐요.

(2)   Q: (한국어 수업에 가다) _____

A: _____

짐 챙기다 ~ topack
(suitcase)

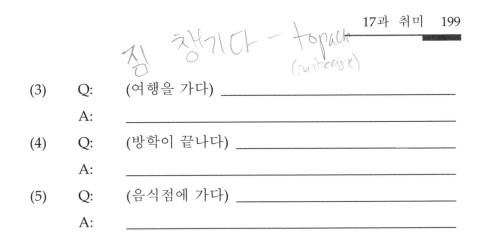

(3)　Q:　(여행을 가다) _____

　　　A:　_____

(4)　Q:　(방학이 끝나다) _____

　　　A:　_____

(5)　Q:　(음식점에 가다) _____

　　　A:　_____

4. Look at the following pictures and describe the events in sequence, using ~기 전에.

Example:　　(1)-(2) 아침 먹기 전에 샤워해요.
　　　　　　(2)-(3) 설겆이 하기 전에 아침 먹어요.

(1)

(2)

(3)

(4)

숟가지

(5)

(6)

양치하다

(7)

(8)

(9)

(10)

GRAMMAR

G17.1   (An act of)~ing: ~는 것

Examples

[Written]

(1)   한국 사람들은 **노래하는 것**을 좋아합니다.

(2)   지하철로 학교에 **가는 것**이 편리합니다.

[Colloquial]

(3)   A: **쇼핑하는 거** 좋아하세요?   Do you like
                                                          shopping?
        B: 아니요, 별로 안 좋아해요.   No, not really.

(4)   A: 일요일 아침에는 뭐 **하는 걸** 좋아해요 ?
        B: **자는 게** 제일 좋아요.

Notes

1. The construction [verb stem~는 것] occurs when verbs need to be expressed as nouns as in the English equivalent 'verb stem~ing'. The dependent noun 것 follows the verb form that is used as a modifier to express an action. Depending on the sentence, a particle (이, 을, 는, 하고 . . .) may be attached to 것. The construction has both a full form, used in writing, and an abbreviated form, used colloquially.

Full form	Abbreviated form
~는 것이	~는 게
~는 것을	~는 걸
~는 것	~는 거
~는 것은	~는 건

2. Nominalizers 'verb stem~기' and 'verb stem~는 것', similar in their function to English gerund (verb stem~ing), can be interchangeable in some cases (G16.2), but, in most cases, ~기 is exclusively used for such fixed expressions as 읽기, 쓰기, and 말하기.

Exercises

1. Answer the following questions:

(1) 주말에는 뭐 하는 걸 좋아하세요?

_____

(2) 노래하는 게 재미있어요?

_____

(3) 지하철을 타는 게 편리해요, 버스를 타는 게 편리해요?

_____

(4) 한국어 공부하는 게 힘들지 않아요?

_____

(5) 방학에 여행하는 걸 좋아해요?

_____

2. What does each person like to do?

(1) 민지   (2) 우진   (3) 스티브

(4) 마이클   (5) 제니   (6) 마크

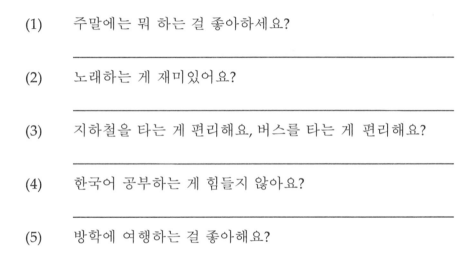

(7) 박 교수님   (8) 유미   (9) 리사

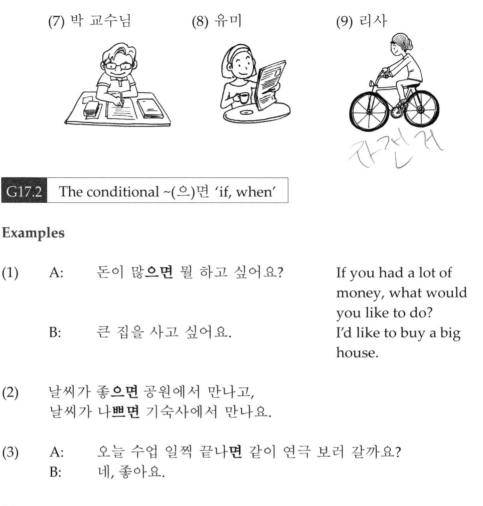

자전거

G17.2   The conditional ~(으)면 'if, when'

Examples

(1)   A: 돈이 많**으면** 뭘 하고 싶어요?   If you had a lot of
                                                    money, what would
                                                    you like to do?

       B: 큰 집을 사고 싶어요.   I'd like to buy a big
                                                    house.

(2)   날씨가 좋**으면** 공원에서 만나고,
       날씨가 나**쁘면** 기숙사에서 만나요.

(3)   A: 오늘 수업 일찍 끝나**면** 같이 연극 보러 갈까요?
       B: 네, 좋아요.

Notes

1. Use of ~(으)면 creates a conditional sentence. In addition to expressing
a condition, as in (1), it can also mean 'when', as in (3). This construction
occurs with various types of main clauses: statements, questions,
requests, and suggestions.

2. ~으면 occurs when the verb stem ends in a consonant other than 르. In
all other environments the form is ~면.

consonant~으면		/ㄹ/ or vowel~면	
먹다	먹으면	가다	가면
받다	받으면	오다	오면
듣다	들으면	살다	살면
춥다	추우면	멀다	멀면

Exercises

1. Turn the verb in parentheses into a conditional.

    (1)   비가 (오다) _____ 우산을 써야 돼요.

    (2)   내일 날씨가 (좋다) _____ 놀러 갈래요?

    (3)   답을 (모르다) _____ 선생님께 물어 보세요.

    (4)   감기에 (걸리다) _____ 따뜻한 물을 많이 드세요.

    (5)   제 이메일을 (받다) _____ 연락 주시겠어요?

    (6)   방이 (더럽다) _____ 청소해야 돼요.

2. Interview your classmates.

    (1)   백만 ('million') 달러가 있으면 무엇을 하고 싶으세요?

    (2)   대학원에 가고 싶으면 어떻게 해요?

    (3)   식당에서 음식이 맛없으면 어떻게 하세요?

    (4)   돈을 다 쓰면 어떻게 해요?

3. Finish the following sentences:

    (1)   시험을 보고 싶지 않으면 _____

    (2)   밤에 배가 고프면 _____

    (3)   수업 시간에 화장실에 가고 싶으면 _____

    (4)   머리가 아프면 _____

G17.3   The comparative 보다 (더) 'more than'

Examples

(1)   A: 갈비가 냉면**보다** 비싸지요?   *Kalbi* is more
                                                    expensive than
                                                    naengmyŏn, isn't it?
      B: 그럼요. 갈비가 **더** 비싸요.   Yes, *kalbi* is more
                                                    expensive.

(2)   A: 백화점에 버스를 타고 갈까요?
      B: 버스**보다** 지하철이 **더** 빨라요.

(3)   A: 순두부찌개와 된장찌개 **중에서** 어느 것을 더 좋아하세요?
      B: 저는 된장찌개를 **더** 좋아해요.

(4)   A: 미국 어디에 한국사람들이 **제일** 많아요?
      B: 로스앤젤레스하고 뉴욕에 **제일** 많이 살아요.

Notes

The comparative construction in Korean employs the particle 보다
'(rather) than' and the adverbs 더 'more' and 덜 'less'. Like all other
particles, 보다 follows the noun being compared (e.g., 책보다 '(rather)
than a book', 불고기보다 '(rather) than *pulgogi*). Word order between the
two nouns being compared is free, and the adverb 더 can be omitted as
shown in (1A). 중에서 'between, among' can also be used as needed as
shown in (3).

> B보다 A가 더 / A가 B보다 더   'A is more than B'
> 냉면보다 갈비가 더 비싸요. = 갈비가 냉면보다 더 비싸요.

> B 보다 A가 덜/ A가 B보다 덜   'A is less than B'
> 갈비보다 냉면이 덜 비싸요. = 냉면이 갈비보다 덜 비싸요.

Comparison in questions has the following word order: nouns being
compared + question word + adjective.

이 두 사람 중에서 누가 더 커요?	Between these two people, who is taller?
한국어와 영어 중에서 어느 것이 더 어려워요?	Between Korean and English which is more difficult?
테니스하고 골프 중에서 어느 것이 더 쉬워요?	Between tennis and golf, which is easier?

Superlative constructions use 제일 or, in writing, 가장.

이 책이 제일 비싸요.	This book is the most expensive.
제일 노래 잘 하는 가수는 누구예요?	Who is the best singer?
미국에서 가장 살고 싶은 도시는 어디입니까?	Which American city do you want to live in the most?

Exercises

1. Compare the following items:

(1)   한국어, 영어 :   _____

(2)   지하철, 버스 :   _____

(3)   뉴욕, 밴쿠버 :   _____

(4)   미국, 호주 :   _____

(5)   의사, 교수 :   _____

(6)   커피, 녹차: _____

(7)   여름, 겨울 :   _____

(8)   여자, 남자 :   _____

2. Compare the prices and say which one is more expensive and by how much.

(1)   불고기 $18   갈비 $21

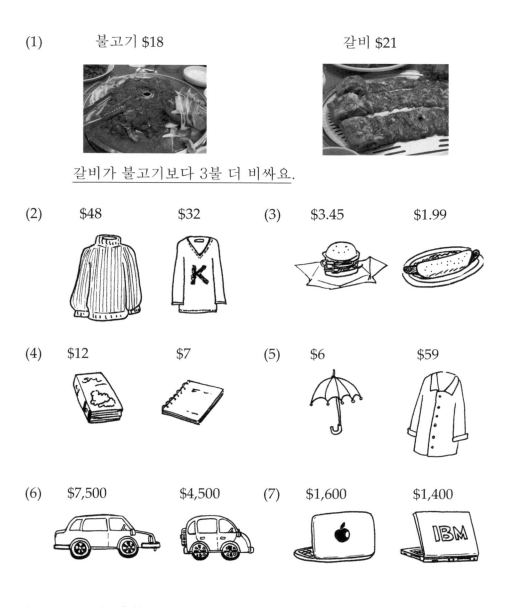

갈비가 불고기보다 3불 더 비싸요.

(2) $48 $32   (3) $3.45 $1.99

(4) $12 $7   (5) $6 $59

(6) $7,500 $4,500   (7) $1,600 $1,400

3. Answer the following questions:

  (1)   백화점보다 물건이 더 싼 곳은 어디예요?

  (2)   한국어보다 쉬운 과목은 어느 것이에요?

  (3)   스타워즈보다 더 재미있는 영화는 뭐예요?

  (4)   불고기와 갈비 중에서 어느 것이 더 맛있어요?

  (5)   한국어와 중국어 중에서 어느 것이 더 배우기 어려울까요?

4. Ask your partner the following questions:

    (1)   제일 좋아하는 음식이 뭐에요?

    (2)   음료수 중에서 뭐를 제일 좋아해요?

    (3)   학교 근처 식당 중에서 어디가 제일 서비스가 좋아요?

    (4)   제일 잘 만들 수 있는 음식이 뭐에요?

Conversation 2   운동 좋아하세요?

(Minji and Steve are talking in the classroom before the class starts.)

민지: 스티브 씨는 무슨 운동 좋아하세요?

스티브: 저는 운동은 다 좋아하지만 특히 테니스를
            자주 쳐요.

민지: 테니스는 언제부터 치기 시작하셨어요?

스티브: 어렸을 때부터요. G17.4

            민지 씨도 테니스 칠 줄 아세요? G17.5

민지: 아니요, 전 테니스 못 쳐요.

            배우고 싶었는데 못 배웠어요.

            저 좀 가르쳐 줄 수 있으세요?

스티브: 그럼 이번 주말에 같이 한번 해 보실래요?

민지: 그럴까요?

스티브: 토요일 2 시 어때요?

민지: 저는 토요일보다 일요일이 좋은데요.

스티브: 그럼 일요일 두 시에 학교 테니스장에서
            만나요.

민지: 네, 좋아요.

전혀 안해요 - not at all
한 번도 안 했어요 - not even once
산책하다 - to walk around / stroll

17과 취미   209

NEW WORDS

NOUN		ADJECTIVE	
기타	guitar	심심하다	to be bored
대답	answer	어리다 (어렸을)	to be young
때	time	**VERB**	
악기	musical instrument	스키 타다	to ski
요리	cooking	조심하다	to be careful
음악회	concert	치다	to play (piano, guitar)
중학교	middle school		
축구	soccer	**ADVERB**	
태권도	Korean martial art	특히	particularly
피아노	piano	**SUFFIX**	
한글	Korean alphabet	~(으)ㄹ 줄	how to

NEW EXPRESSIONS

박물관

살찌다

1. 시작하다 is a transitive verb that means 'to begin something', as in
수업을 시작합니다. ~기 시작하다 follows a verb stem. The nominalizer
~기 (G16.2) and the preceding verb stem form a nominalized
construction, which functions as the object of the transitive verb 시작하다.

Examples:

A:　언제부터 축구를 하기 시작했어요?　(From) when did you begin
　　　　　　　　　　　　　　　　　　playing soccer?

B:　작년부터 다시 하기 시작했어요.　I began playing again (since)
　　　　　　　　　　　　　　　　　last year.

2. Sports activities:

하다

농구하다	to play basketball	축구하다	to play soccer
야구하다	to play baseball	조깅하다	to jog

하다/가다

여행하다	to travel	등산하다	to hike
여행 가다	to go traveling	등산 가다	to go hiking

치다

골프 치다   to play golf   테니스 치다   to play tennis

타다

스키 타다   to ski   자전거 타다   to ride bicycles

Exercises

1. List all the names of the sports you know in Korean.

2. Fill in the blanks based on conversation 2.

      (1)   스티브는 _____을 다 좋아합니다.

      (2)   스티브는 _____ 때부터 테니스를 치기 시작했습니다.

      (3)   민지는 테니스를 못 _____ 봤습니다.

      (4)   이번 _____에 민지와 스티브는 학교 _____
에서 만날 겁니다.

3. Complete the sentences as shown.

      (1)   5분 전, 비가 오다
            5분 전부터 비가 오기 시작했어요.

      (2)   지난 주, 수영을 하다

      (3)   3월, 로스앤젤레스에 살다

      (4)   3년 전, 대학원에 다니다

      (5)   첫 학기, 친구들을 사귀다

      (6)   겨울 방학, 태권도를 배우다

GRAMMAR

| G17.4 | N 때 'at the time of N'; ~(으)ㄹ 때 'when' |

Examples

(1)   중학교 **때** 무슨 과목이 제일 재미있었어요?

(2)   A: 초등학교 **때** 어디서 살았어요?
      B: 열살 **때**까지 서울에서 살았어요.

(3)   A: 공부**할 때** 음악을 들으세요?   Do you listen to music
                                          when you study?
      B: 저는 **공부할 때** 다른 일을   When I study, I can't do
           못 해요.   other things.

(4)   A: **심심할 때** 뭐 해요?
      B: 컴퓨터 게임도 하고 음악도 들어요.

(5)   **어렸을 때** 제주도(Cheju Island)에 가 봤어요.

Notes

1. [Noun 때] refers to the duration of the event, activity, or process
denoted by the noun. Nouns that do not themselves indicate time may be
followed by 때 as in 올림픽('Olympics Game') 때 and 시험 때. However,
time-indicating expressions such as 아침, 주말, and 작년 are combined
with the temporal particle 에 instead as in 아침에, 주말에, 작년에, 밤에,
일월에, 가을에.
        For some expressions such as 아침, 점심, 저녁, and 방학, both
때 and 에 can be used. 아침 때 means 'at the time of morning/breakfast'
whereas 아침에 means 'in the morning'.

2. ~(으)ㄹ 때 is used with a verb or an adjective when two events overlap
in time. For example, in (3A), the event of "studying" and the event of
"listening to music" overlap. ~때 is used with a noun as in examples (1)
and (2).

Additional grammar points: Although ~(으)면 (G17.2) also means 'when' (in addition to its conditional meaning), ~(으)면 and ~(으)ㄹ 때 differ. ~(으)ㄹ 때 deals only with time; ~(으)면 expresses an inherent relationship between the two clauses. For example, 겨울이 될 때 눈이 와요 is less natural here than 겨울이 되면 눈이 와요 because there is a close relationship between the season and the weather, and thus the second is preferred.

Exercises

1. Fill in the blanks with either 때 or 에.

(1)   방학_때_   (2)   주말_____

(3)   학기말_____   (4)   대학교_____

(5)   봄_____   (6)   시험_____

2. Change the verbs or adjectives in parentheses to show that the two events/activities/processes are concurrent.

(1)   (스키 타다) 때 조심하세요.

       스키 탈 때 조심하세요.

(2)   (숙제하다) 때 음악을 들어요?

       숙제 할 때 _____

(3)   돈이 (없다) 때 친구한테 전화를 해요.

       없을 _____

(4)   처음 대학교에 (오다) 때 친구가 한 명도 없었어요.

       올 왔을 _____

(5)   날씨가 (춥다) 때 스웨터를 자주 입어요.

       추울 _____

(6)   대답을 (모르다) 때 선생님께 질문해요.

       모을 _____

(7)   음악회에 (가다) 때 무슨 옷을 입어요?

       갈 _____

3. Ask your partner these questions and report the responses to your class.

    (1)   시험 때 몇 시까지 공부해요?

         _____

    (2)   지난 봄 방학 때 뭐 했어요?

         _____

    (3)   이번 여름 방학 때 뭐 할 거예요?

         _____

    (4)   학교에 올 때 누구하고 같이 와요?

         _____

    (5)   어렸을 때 어디에서 살았어요?

         _____

    (6)   고등학교 다닐 때 무슨 운동 좋아했어요?

         _____

| G17.5 | ~(으)ㄹ 줄 알다/모르다 'know/not know how to' |

Examples

(1)   A: 태권도 할 **줄 아세요?**   Do you know how to do Taekwondo?

       B: 네, 할 **줄 알아요.**   Yes, I do.

(2)   A: 한글을 **읽을 줄 알**면 한국 노래를 가르쳐 줄 수 있으세요?

       B: 네, 가르쳐 드릴게요.

(3)   저는 바이올린은 **켤 줄 알**지만 피아노는 못 쳐요.

Notes

1. ~(으)ㄹ 줄 알다/모르다 'know/not know how to' specifically refers to
the ability or the way to do something, while ~(으)ㄹ 수 있다/없다
'can/cannot' refers to a wide range of possibilities and abilities (G15.1).
Consider the following examples:

운전 할 줄 알지만 지금은 피곤해서 운전 할 수 없어요. (or 지금은 운전을 못 해요).	I know how to drive, but I cannot drive right now because I am tired.
테니스는 칠 줄 알지만 시간이 없어서 오늘은 칠 수 없어요.	I know how to play tennis, but I cannot play today because I don't have time.

Exercises

1. Find someone in the classroom who fits the following descriptions:

(1)   스키를 탈 줄 아는 사람

(2)   운전을 할 줄 모르는 사람 —

(3)   기타를 칠 줄 아는 여자 — simon

(4)   요리를 할 줄 아는 남자 — Royce

(5)   축구를 할 줄 아는 사람 — rachel

2. Interview your partner.

(1)   배가 고프지요? 무슨 음식을 만들 줄 알아요?

(2)   무슨 운동을 할 줄 아세요?

(3)   무슨 노래를 할 줄 아세요?

(4)   어떤 악기를 연주할 줄 아세요?

(5)   어느 나라 말을 할 줄 알아요? 중국어를 할 줄 알아요?

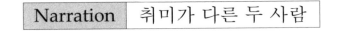

Narration 취미가 다른 두 사람

수빈이와 수빈이의 남자 친구 현우는 취미가 아주
다릅니다. 수빈이는 음악을 좋아하고 운동을 싫어하지만,
현우는 운동을 좋아하고 음악을 별로 좋아하지 않습니다.
지난 토요일에 음악회에 갔는데 현우가 피아노 연주
시간에 잠만 잤습니다. 이번 주말에도 두 사람은 서로
다른 것을 하고 싶어합니다. 수빈이는 새로 나온 영화를
보고 싶어하고, 현우는 축구 경기[1]를 보고 싶어합니다.
그래서 '가위 바위 보'[2]를 했습니다. 현우가 이기면[3]
축구를 보러 가고 수빈이가 이기면 영화를 보는 것으로
했습니다. 현우가 졌기[4] 때문에 두 사람은 영화를
봤습니다.

1. 축구 경기: soccer game
2. 가위 바위 보: rock-paper-scissors
3. 이기다: to win
4. 지다: to lose

NEW EXPRESSIONS

1. 서로 'each other, mutually'

수빈과 현우는 서로 좋아합니다.　　Soobin and Hyunwoo like
　　　　　　　　　　　　　　　　　each other.

서로 이야기해 보세요.　　　　　　Please talk to each other.

2. 가위, 바위, 보 'rock-paper-scissors' is a game that originated in Asia. 가위 'scissors' can beat 보 'paper, cloth wrapper' because it can cut the paper or cloth, but it is helpless in the presence of 바위 'rock'. However, 보 can wrap 바위 and render it helpless. Often decisions are made and winners are chosen on the basis of this game.

가위　　　　　　바위　　　　　　보

3. 이기다 means 'to win, beat'. The opposite is 지다 'to lose'. Examples:

한국 축구팀이 일본 팀을　　　　The Korean soccer team beat
3대 1로 이겼어요.　　　　　　　the Japanese team by 3 to 1.

이태리가 프랑스한테 졌어요.　　Italy was defeated by France.

Exercises

1. Fill in the blanks based on the narration.

(1)　　　수빈은 ＿＿＿＿＿을 좋아하지만 ＿＿＿＿＿은
　　　　　싫어합니다.

(2)　　　현우는 수빈의 ＿＿＿＿＿ 친구예요.

(3)　　　수빈과 현우는 ＿＿＿＿＿ 토요일에 ＿＿＿＿＿에
　　　　　갔습니다.

(4)   수빈은 이번 주말에 _____ 나온 영화를 _____
      싶어합니다.

(5)   현우는 _____를 _____고 싶어합니다.

(6)   수빈과 현우는 취미가 아주 _____.

(7)   그래서 _____ 바위 보를 해서 _____ 사람이
      하고 싶은 것을 하기로 했습니다.

2. Connect the corresponding words.

(1)   음악회   •   •   자다

(2)   자전거   •   •   하다

(3)   영화   •   •   가다

(4)   가위 바위 보   •   •   타다

(5)   잠   •   •   보다

CULTURE

축구, 야구, 씨름, 그리고 태권도 (Soccer, baseball, Ssirŭm, and Taekwondo)

Like people in many other countries in the world, Koreans enjoy diverse sports. Soccer is one of the most popular sports in Korea. The Korea-Japan World Cup in 2002, for example, benchmarked a sensational development in soccer fandom. People came out to the streets to root for the Korean team wearing red, which symbolizes 붉은 악마 (Red Devils), a self-given name for soccer fans in Korea.

Another 붉은 악마 experience hit the country during the World Baseball Classic in 2009. In the tournament, Korea made it to the finals, competing against such strong opponents as the United States, Japan, and Cuba. Many baseball players have been making the excitement double for baseball fans with their outstanding performance in foreign professional leagues.

Korean traditional sports, on the other hand, represent other values and meanings than popularity. 씨름, for example, is a sport of traditional holidays. It is a kind of wrestling where two people match their strength and skills on a sand ring. Anyone who touches the ground with other than their feet loses the game. Usually, the winner of the competition is awarded a miniature golden bull. 태권도 is another traditional sport that is widely practiced in Korea. The traditional martial art, rather than

being a popular sport, is valued as a way to train your body and spirit. Many people learn it from childhood, and men are trained in it once again when they join the military.

USAGE

A. Talking about favorite activities

It is usual to ask about another person's hobbies or favorite activities.

(1)   A: 뭐 하는 걸 좋아하세요?
       B: 저는 등산하는 걸 좋아해요.

(2)   A: 취미가 뭐예요?
       B: 우표도 모으고 시계도 모아요. (모으다 'to collect')

(3)   A: 운동 좋아하세요?
       B: 아주 좋아해요. 보는 것도 좋아하고 하는 것도 좋아해요. 올림픽('Olympic') 게임을 보는 게 재미있어요.

(4) A: 일요일에는 보통 뭐 하세요?
  B: 게임 해요. 게임을 하면 시간이 아주 빨리 가요.

(5) A: 어떤 음악을 좋아하세요?
  B: 음악을 다 좋아하지만 특히 재즈 음악을 좋아해요.

(6) A: 여행 좋아하세요?
  B: 네, 한국에서 안 가 본 곳이 없어요.
    특히 설악산(Mt. Seol-ak)이 좋았어요.

(7) A: 영화 자주 보러 가세요?
  B: 극장에는 별로 안 가지만 DVD는 많이 빌려 봐요.

Exercises

1. Ask your partner if he or she likes the following activities. If so, ask how often he or she does them.

보기: 크로스워드 퍼즐 'crossword puzzle'

  Q: 크로스워드 퍼즐 하는 걸 좋아하세요?
  A: 네, 좋아해요. 보통 룸메이트하고 같이 해요.
  Q: 얼마나 자주 하세요?
  A: 일주일에 한 번 정도 해요. 일요일 아침에 일어나서
    커피 마시면서 신문에 나온 것을 해요.

---

(1) 책 읽기 (2) 노래방에 가기
(3) 태권도 하기 (4) 음악 듣기
(5) 자전거 타기 (6) 그림 그리기

2. Interview your classmates and compile statistics for each question. Present your findings to the class.

(1) 좋아하는 가수가 누구예요? 그 가수의 음악회에
    가 봤어요?

(2) 그림을 보는 걸 좋아하세요? 어디에 가서 그림을 보았어요?

(3)   올림픽에서 무슨 스포츠를 열심히 봅니까?

(4)   춤추러 어느 클럽에 자주 갑니까?

3. Interview your classmates.

(1)   피아노(골프, 테니스 . . .)를 칠 줄 알아요? 언제부터 배우기
시작했어요?

(2)   언제부터 한국말을 공부하기 시작했어요?

(3)   한국에서는 겨울에 보통 언제부터 눈이 오기 시작해요?

(4)   남자/여자 친구 있어요? 언제부터 만나기 시작했어요?

B. Describing feelings

기분이 좋다	A: B:	시험이 다 끝났지요? 네, 오늘 아침에 끝났어요. 기분이 정말 좋아요.
기분이 나쁘다	A: B:	왜 기분이 나빠요? 잠을 못 자서 몸이 안 좋아요.

슬프다 'to be sad'

행복하다 'to be happy'

화가 나다 'to be angry'

피곤하다 'to be tired'

무섭다 'to be afraid'

신나다 'to be excited'

좋다 'to like'

싫다 'to dislike'

심심하다 'to feel bored'

Exercises

1. Answer the questions.

(1)   언제 제일 기분이 좋았어요?

_____

(2)   어느 영화가 슬퍼요? 보면서 운 (울다 'to cry')
영화가 있어요?

_____

(3)   룸메이트가 화가 났을 때 어떻게 해요?

_____

(4)   심심할 때 보통 뭘 해요?

_____

(5)   뭐가 무서워요?

_____

(6)   언제 스트레스('stress')를 받아요?

_____

(7)   피곤하면 뭘 해요?

_____

2. Give two examples for each category.

(1)   기분이 좋은 사람   시험을 잘 본 사람
데이트('date')하는 사람

(2)   화가 난 사람   _____

_____

(3)   신나는 음악   _____

_____

(4)   슬픈 책   _____

_____

(5)   싫은 과일 ('fruit')   _____

_____

(6)   행복한 사람   _____

_____

Lesson 17 - Hobbies

CONVERSATION 1: What are your hobbies?
(Mark and Minji meet at a party.)

Mark:	Minji, what are your hobbies?
Minji:	I enjoy drawing. How about you, Mark?
Mark:	I love music.
Minji:	What kind of music do you enjoy?
Mark:	I like classical music. Especially the strings, like the violin. Whenever I listen to the violin, it puts me in a good mood. That's why I listen to some violin music before going to bed.
	Minji, do you also enjoy music?
Minji:	I prefer rock or jazz to classical music.
Mark:	Isn't rock a little bit noisy?
Minji:	Yes, it is. My roommate hates it when I pump up the volume. So I got a new set of headphones last week.

CONVERSATION 2: Do you like sports?
(Minji and Steve are talking in the classroom before the class starts.)

Minji:	Steve, what kind of sports do you like?
Steve:	I like all sports, but I play a lot of tennis.
Minji:	When did you start playing tennis?
Steve:	[I started] when I was a little kid. Do you also play tennis, Minji?
Minji:	No, I don't. I've always wanted to learn it but never had a chance. Can you teach me?
Steve:	Would you like to try this weekend?
Minji:	Can I?
Steve:	How about Saturday two o'clock?
Minji:	Sunday is better than Saturday for me.
Steve:	Okay, then, let's meet at the school tennis court Sunday two o'clock.
Minji:	All right.

NARRATION: A couple with different hobbies

Soobin and her boyfriend Hyunwoo have very different hobbies. Soobin enjoys music and dislikes sports; Hyunwoo likes sports and doesn't care for music. Last Saturday they went to a recital, but Hyunwoo fell asleep while listening to the piano performance. Even this weekend, the two of them want to do different things. Soobin wants to go to see a new movie while Hyunwoo wants to go to a soccer match. They did a rock-paper-scissors to decide what to do. If Hyunwoo won, they'd go to the soccer game; if Soobin won, they'd go to see a movie. Since Hyunwoo lost, they went to the movies.

Appendices

Appendix 1-1. Copula, Adjective, and Verb Conjugations

Lesson	Dictionary form / Patterns	이다	아니다	있다	계시다	되다	하다 Adjective: 깨끗하다 / Verb: 공부하다
G12.2 G13.5	~겠어요 polite	-	-	있겠어요	계시겠어요	되겠어요	깨끗하겠어요 / 공부하겠어요
G7.3	~고 clausal connective	(이)고	아니고	있고	계시고	되고	깨끗하고 / 공부하고
G15.5	~고 나서 clausal connective	-	-	-	-	되고 나서	- / 공부하고 나서
G10.2	~고 싶다/싶어하다 expressing desire	-	-	있고 싶다/싶어하다	계시고 싶어하다	되고 싶다/싶어하다	- / 공부하고 싶다/싶어하다
G11.1	~고 있다 progressive	-	-	-	-	되고 있다	- / 공부하고 있다
G16.3	~기 때문에 clausal connective	(이)기 때문에	아니기 때문에	있기 때문에	계시기 때문에	되기 때문에	깨끗하기 때문에 / 공부하기 때문에
G9.2	~(으)ㄴ noun modifier	인	아닌	-	-	-	깨끗한 / -
G12.5	~(으)ㄴ noun modifier (past)	-	-	-	계신	된	- / 공부한
G10.1	~(으)ㄴ데 background information	인데	아닌데	-	-	-	깨끗한데 / -
G10.5	~는 noun modifier	-	-	있는	계시는	되는	- / 공부하는

Lesson	Dictionary form / Patterns	이다	아니다	있다	계시다	되다	하다 Adjective: 깨끗하다 / Verb: 공부하다
G10.1	~는데 background information	-	-	있는데	계시는데	되는데	- / 공부하는데
G12.3	~네요 sentence ending	(이)네요	아니네요	있네요	계시네요	되네요	깨끗하네요 / 공부하네요
G15.4	~(으)ㄹ noun modifier (prospective)	일	아닐	있을	계실	될	- / 공부할
G7.1	~(으)ㄹ 거예요 probability	일 거예요	아닐 거예요	있을 거예요	계실 거예요	될 거예요	깨끗할 거예요 / 공부할 거예요
G13.3	~(으)ㄹ게요 'I will' (willingness)	-	-	있을게요	-	될게요	- / 공부할게요
G11.4	~(으)ㄹ까요? asking opinion	일까요?	아닐까요?	있을까요?	계실까요?	될까요?	깨끗할까요? / 공부할까요?
G17.4	~(으)ㄹ 때 'when'	일 때	아닐 때	있을 때	계실 때	될 때	깨끗할 때 / 공부할 때
G11.2	~(으)ㄹ래요 intention	-	-	있을래요 있을래요?	계실래요?	될래요 될래요?	- / 공부할래요
G15.1	~(으)ㄹ 수 있다/없다 possibility/ ability	일 수 있다/없다	아닐 수 있다/없다	있을 수 있다/없다	계실 수 있다/없다	될 수 있다/없다	깨끗할 수 있다/없다 / 공부할 수 있다/없다
G17.5	~(으)ㄹ 줄 알다/모르다 'know/not know how to'	-	-	-	-	-	- / 공부할 줄 알다/모르다

Lesson	Dictionary form / Patterns	이다	아니다	있다	계시다	되다	하다 Adjective: 깨끗하다 / Verb: 공부하다
G5.3	~(으)러 purpose	-	-	-	-	-	- / 공부하러
G17.2	~(으)면 conditional	(이)면	아니면	있으면	계시면	되면	깨끗하면 / 공부하면
G15.3	~(으)면서 'while ~ing'	이면서	아니면서	있으면서	계시면서	되면서	깨끗하면서 / 공부하면서
G3.2	~(으)세요 honorific polite	(이)세요	아니세요	있으세요	계세요	되세요	깨끗하세요 / 공부하세요
G9.4	~(으)셨어요 honorific polite (past)	(이)셨어요	아니셨어요	있으셨어요	계셨어요	되셨어요	깨끗하셨어요 / 공부하셨어요
G8.3	~(으)셨습니다 honorific deferential (past)	(이)셨습니다	아니셨습니다	있으셨습니다	계셨습니다	되셨습니다	깨끗하셨습니다 / 공부하셨습니다
G8.3	~습니다/까? ~ㅂ니다/까? deferential	입니다/ 입니까?	아닙니다/ 아닙니까?	있습니다/ 있습니까?	계십니다/ 계십니까?	됩니다/ 됩니까?	깨끗합니다/ 깨끗합니까? / 공부합니다/ 공부합니까?
G8.3	~(으)십니다/ (으)십니까? honorific deferential	(이)십니다/ (이)십니까?	아니십니다/ 아니십니까?	있으십니다/ 있으십니까?	계십니다/ 계십니까?	되십니다/ 되십니까?	깨끗하십니다/ 깨끗하십니까? / 공부하십니다/ 공부하십니까?
G16.1	~어/아 보다 'try doing'	-	-	있어 보다	계셔 보다	되어 보다 /돼 보다	- / 공부해 보다
G10.4 G12.1	~어서/아서 causal, sequential clausal conn.	(이)라서 /이어서 /여서	아니라서/ 아니어서	있어서	계셔서	되어서 /돼서	깨끗해서 / 공부해서
G2.5	~어요/아요 polite	이에요 /예요	아니에요	있어요	계세요	되어요 /돼요	깨끗해요 / 공부해요

Lesson	Dictionary form / Patterns	이다	아니다	있다	계시다	되다	하다 Adjective: 깨끗하다 / Verb: 공부하다
G13.2	~어/아야 되다 obligation, necessity	이어야/ 여야 되다	아니어야 되다	있어야 되다	계셔야 되다	되어야 되다 /돼야 되다	깨끗해야 되다 / 공부해야 되다
G13.1	~어/아 주다 /드리다 benefactive	-	-	있어 주다 /드리다	계셔 주다	되어 주다 /드리다	- / 공부해 주다 /드리다
G10.1	~었/았는데 background information (past)	이었는데 /였는데	아니었는데	있었는데	계셨는데	되었는데	깨끗했는데 / 공부했는데
G8.3	~었/았습니다 deferential (past)	이었습니다 /였습니다	아니었습니다	있었습니다	계셨습니다	되었습니다	깨끗했습니다 / 공부했습니다
G6.3	~었/았/ 쓰어요 polite (past)	이었어요 /였어요	아니었어요	있었어요	계셨어요	되었어요	깨끗했어요 / 공부했어요
G14.4	~지 마세요 negative command	-	-	있지 마세요	계시지 마세요	되지 마세요	- / 공부하지 마세요
G9.5	~지만 'but, although'	(이)지만	아니지만	있지만	계시지만	되지만	깨끗하지만 / 공부하지만
G14.2	~지 못하다 'cannot' long negation			있지 못하다	계시지 못하다	되지 못하다	깨끗하지 못하다 / 공부하지 못하다
G16.5	~지 않다 'do not' long negation	-	-	있지 않다	계시지 않다	되지 않다	깨끗하지 않다 / 공부하지 않다
G8.1	~지요? seeking agreement	(이)지요?	아니지요?	있지요?	계시지요?	되지요?	깨끗하지요? / 공부하지요?

Appendix 1-2. Conjugation of Irregular Adjectives and Verbs

Lesson	Dictionary form / Patterns	-ㄷ 듣다 걷다 묻다	-ㄹ Adjective: 멀다, 길다 Verb: 열다, 팔다, 놀다, 돌다, 만들다, 살다, 알다	-ㅂ Adjective: 춥다, 덥다, 쉽다, 어렵다, 반갑다, 즐겁다 Verb: 돕다
G12.2 G13.2	~겠어요 polite	듣겠어요	멀겠어요 열겠어요	춥겠어요 돕겠어요
G7.3	~고 clausal connective	듣고	멀고 열고	춥고 돕고
G15.5	~고 나서 clausal connective	듣고 나서	- 열고 나서	- 돕고 나서
G10.2	~고 싶다/싶어하다 expressing desire	듣고 싶다 듣고 싶어하다	- 열고 싶다 열고 싶어하다	- 돕고 싶다 돕고 싶어하다
G11.1	~고 있다 progressive	듣고 있다	- 열고 있다	- 돕고 있다
G16.3	~기 때문에 clausal connective	듣기 때문에	멀기 때문에 열기 때문에	춥기 때문에 돕기 때문에
G9.2	~(으)ㄴ noun modifier	-	먼 -	추운 -
G12.5	~(으)ㄴ noun modifier (past)	들은	- 연	- 도운
G10.1	~(으)ㄴ데 background information	-	먼데 -	추운데 -
G10.5	~는 noun modifier	듣는	- 여는	- 돕는

Lesson	Dictionary form / Patterns	-ㅎ 그렇다 이렇다 저렇다 빨갛다 노랗다 파랗다 하얗다	-으 Adjective: 크다, 바쁘다 Verb: 쓰다	-르 Adjective: 다르다, 빠르다 Verb: 부르다, 모르다
G12.2 G13.2	~겠어요 polite	그렇겠어요	크겠어요 쓰겠어요	다르겠어요 부르겠어요
G7.3	~고 clausal connective	그렇고	크고 쓰고	다르고 부르고
G15.5	~고 나서 clausal connective	그러고 나서	– 쓰고 나서	– 부르고 나서
G10.2	~고 싶다/싶어하다 expressing desire	그러고 싶다/ 그러고 싶어하다	– 쓰고 싶다/ 쓰고 싶어하다	– 부르고 싶다/ 부르고 싶어하다
G11.1	~고 있다 progressive	그러고 있다	– 쓰고 있다	– 부르고 있다
G16.3	~기 때문에 clausal connective	그렇기 때문에	크기 때문에 쓰기 때문에	다르기 때문에 부르기 때문에
G9.2	Adjective ~(으)ㄴ noun modifier	그런	큰 -	다른 -
G12.5	Verb ~(으)ㄴ noun modifier (past)	-	– 쓴	– 부른
G10.1	Adjective ~(으)ㄴ데 background information	그런데	큰데 -	다른데 -
G10.5	Verb ~는 noun modifier	–	– 쓰는	– 부르는

Lesson	Dictionary form / Patterns	-ㄷ 듣다 걷다 묻다	-ㄹ Adjective: 멀다, 길다 Verb: 열다, 팔다, 놀다, 돌다, 만들다, 살다, 알다	-ㅂ Adjective: 춥다, 덥다, 쉽다, 어렵다, 반갑다, 즐겁다 Verb: 돕다
G10.1	~는데 background information	듣는데	- 여는데	- 돕는데
G12.3	~네요 sentence ending	듣네요	머네요 여네요	춥네요 돕네요
G15.4	~(으)ㄹ noun modifier (prospective)	들을	멀 열	추울 도울
G7.1	~(으)ㄹ 거예요 probability	들을 거예요	멀 거예요 열 거예요	추울 거예요 도울 거예요
G13.3	~(으)ㄹ게요 'I will' (willingness)	들을게요	- 열게요	- 도울게요
G11.4	~(으)ㄹ까요? asking opinion	들을까요?	멀까요? 열까요?	추울까요? 도울까요?
G17.4	~(으)ㄹ 때 'when'	들을 때	멀 때 열 때	추울 때 도울 때
G11.2	~(으)ㄹ래요 intention	들을래요	- 열래요	- 도울래요
G15.1	~(으)ㄹ 수 있다/없다 possibility/ability	들을 수 있다	- 열 수 있다	- 도울 수 있다
G17.5	~(으)ㄹ 줄 알다/모르다 'know/not know how to'	들을 줄 알다	- 열 줄 알다	- 도울 줄 알다

Lesson	Dictionary form / Patterns	-ㅎ 그렇다 이렇다 저렇다 빨갛다 노랗다 파랗다 하얗다	-으 Adjective: 크다, 바쁘다 Verb: 쓰다	-르 Adjective: 다르다, 빠르다 Verb: 부르다, 모르다
G10.1	~는데 background information	그런데	– 쓰는데	– 부르는데
G12.3	~네요 sentence ending	그렇네요	크네요 쓰네요	다르네요 부르네요
G15.4	~(으)ㄹ noun modifier (prospective)	그럴	클 쓸	다를 부를
G7.1	~(으)ㄹ 거예요 probability	그럴 거예요	클 거예요 쓸 거예요	다를 거예요 부를 거예요
G13.3	~(으)ㄹ게요 'I will' (willingness)	그럴게요	– 쓸게요	– 부를게요
G11.4	~(으)ㄹ까요? asking opinion	그럴까요?	클까요? 쓸까요?	다를까요? 부를까요?
G17.4	~(으)ㄹ 때 'when'	그럴 때	클 때 쓸 때	다를 때 부를 때
G11.2	~(으)ㄹ래요 intention	그럴래요	– 쓸래요	– 부를래요
G15.1	~(으)ㄹ 수 있다/없다 possibility/ability	그럴 수 있다	클 수 있다 쓸 수 있다	다를 수 있다 부를 수 있다
G17.5	~(으)ㄹ 줄 알다/모르다 'know/not know how to'	그럴 줄 알다	– 쓸 줄 알다	– 부를 줄 알다

Lesson	Patterns / Dictionary form	-ㄷ 듣다 걷다 묻다	-ㄹ Adjective: 멀다, 길다 Verb: 열다, 팔다, 놀다, 돌다, 만들다, 살다, 알다	-ㅂ Adjective: 춥다, 덥다, 쉽다, 어렵다, 반갑다, 즐겁다 Verb: 돕다
G5.3	~(으)러 purpose	들으러	- 열러	- 도우러
G17.2	~(으)면 conditional	들으면	멀면 열면	추우면 도우면
G15.3	~(으)면서 'while ~ing'	들으면서	멀면서 열면서	추우면서 도우면서
G3.2	~(으)세요 honorific polite	들으세요	머세요 여세요	추우세요 도우세요
G9.4	~(으)셨어요 honorific polite (past)	들으셨어요	머셨어요 여셨어요	추우셨어요 도우셨어요
G8.3	~(으)셨습니다 honorific deferential (past)	들으셨습니다	- 여셨습니다	- 도우셨습니다
G8.3	~습니다/까? ~ㅂ니다/까? deferential	듣습니다/까?	멉니다/까? 엽니다/까?	춥습니다/까? 도웁니다/까?
G8.3	~(으)십니다/ (으)십니까? honorific deferential	들으십니다/까?	머십니다/까? 여십니다/까?	추우십니다/까? 도우십니다/까?
G16.1	~어/아 보다 'try doing'	들어 보다	- 열어 보다	- 도와 보다
G10.4 G12.1	~어서/아서 causal, sequential clausal conn.	들어서	멀어서 열어서	추워서 도와서

Lesson	Dictionary form / Patterns	-ㅎ 그렇다 이렇다 저렇다 빨갛다 노랗다 파랗다 하얗다	-으 Adjective: 크다, 바쁘다 Verb: 쓰다	-르 Adjective: 다르다, 빠르다 Verb: 부르다, 모르다
G5.3	~(으)러 purpose	-	- 쓰러	- 부르러
G17.2	~(으)면 conditional	그러면	크면 쓰면	다르면 부르면
G15.3	~(으)면서 'while ~ing'	그러면서	크면서 쓰면서	다르면서 부르면서
G3.2	~(으)세요 honorific polite	그러세요	크세요 쓰세요	- 부르세요
G9.4	~(으)셨어요 honorific polite (past)	그러셨어요	크셨어요 쓰셨어요	다르셨어요 부르셨어요
G8.3	~(으)셨습니다 honorific deferential (past)	그러셨습니다	크셨습니다 쓰셨습니다	다르셨습니다 부르셨습니다
G8.3	~습니다/까? ~ㅂ니다/까? deferential	그렇습니다/까?	크셨습니다/까? 쓰셨습니다/까?	다릅니다/까? 부릅니다/까?
G8.3	~(으)십니다/ (으)십니까? honorific deferential	그러십니다/까?	크십니다/까? 쓰십니다/까?	다르십니다/까? 부르십니다/까?
G16.1	~어/아 보다 'try doing'	그래 보다	- 써 보다	- 불러 보다
G10.4 G12.1	~어서/아서 causal, sequential clausal conn.	그래서	커서 써서	달라서 불러서

Lesson	Dictionary form \ Patterns	-ㄷ 듣다 걷다 묻다	-ㄹ Adjective: 멀다, 길다 / Verb: 열다, 팔다, 놀다, 돌다, 만들다, 살다, 알다	-ㅂ Adjective: 춥다, 덥다, 쉽다, 어렵다, 반갑다, 즐겁다 / Verb: 돕다
G2.5	~어요/아요 polite	들어요	멀어요 열어요	추워요 도와요
G13.2	~어/아야 되다 obligation, necessity	들어야 되다	멀어야 되다 열어야 되다	추워야 되다 도와야 되다
G13.1	~어/아 주다 /드리다 benefactive	들어 주다/드리다	- 열어 주다/드리다	- 도와 주다/드리다
G10.1	~었/았는데 background information (past)	들었는데	멀었는데 열었는데	추웠는데 도왔는데
G8.3	~었/았습니다 deferential (past)	들었습니다	멀었습니다 열었습니다	추웠습니다 도왔습니다
G6.3	~었/았/ㅆ어요 polite (past)	들었어요	멀었어요 열었어요	추웠어요 도왔어요
G14.4	~지 마세요 negative command	듣지 마세요	- 열지 마세요	- 돕지 마세요
G9.5	~지만 'but, although'	듣지만	멀지만 열지만	춥지만 돕지만
G14.2	~지 못하다 'cannot' long negation	듣지 못하다	- 열지 못하다	- 돕지 못하다
G16.5	~지 않다 'do not' long negation	듣지 않다	멀지 않다 열지 않다	춥지 않다 돕지 않다
G8.1	~지요? seeking agreement	듣지요?	멀지요? 열지요?	춥지요? 돕지요?

Lesson	Dictionary form / Patterns	-ㅎ 그렇다 이렇다 저렇다 빨갛다 노랗다 파랗다 하얗다	-으 Adjective: 크다, 바쁘다 Verb: 쓰다	-르 Adjective: 다르다, 빠르다 Verb: 부르다, 모르다
G2.5	~어요/아요 polite	그래요	커요 / 써요	달라요 / 불러요
G13.2	~어/아야 되다 obligation, necessity	그래야 돼요	커야 돼요 / 써야 돼요	달라야 돼요 / 불러야 돼요
G13.1	~어/아 주다 /드리다 benefactive	-	- / 써 주다/드리다	- / 불러 주다/드리다
G10.1	~었/았는데 background information (past)	그랬는데	컸는데 / 썼는데	달랐는데 / 불렀는데
G8.3	~었/았습니다 deferential (past)	그랬습니다	컸습니다 / 썼습니다	달랐습니다 / 불렀습니다
G6.3	~었/았/ㅆ어요 polite (past)	그랬어요	컸어요 / 썼어요	달랐어요 / 불렀어요
G14.4	~지 마세요 negative command	그러지 마세요	- / 쓰지 마세요	- / 부르지 마세요
G9.5	~지만 'but, although'	그렇지만	크지만 / 쓰지만	다르지만 / 부르지만
G14.2	~지 못하다 'cannot' long negation	그렇지 못하다	- / 쓰지 못하다	- / 부르지 못하다
G16.5	~지 않다 'do not' long negation	그렇지 않다	크지 않다 / 쓰지 않다	다르지 않다 / 부르지 않다
G8.1	~지요? seeking agreement	그렇지요?	크지요? / 쓰지요?	다르지요? / 부르지요?

Appendix 1-3. The Three Types of Conjugation

Conjugations for adjectives and verbs can be classified into the following three types:

   A. stem + 어/아
   B. stem + (으)
   C. no change in stem

A. Stem + 어/아	B. Stem + (으)	C. No change in stem
~어/아 드리다	~(으)ㄴ	~게
~어/아 보다	~(으)ㄴ데	~겠
~어/아 주다	~(으)ㄴ데요	~고
~어/아야 되다	~(으)ㄹ	~고 나서
~어서/아서	~(으)ㄹ 거예요	~고 습니다/ㅂ니다
~어요/아요	~(으)ㄹ 때	~고 습니까/ㅂ니까
~었/았/ㅆ어요	~(으)ㄹ 수	~고 있다
	~(으)ㄹ게요	~고 싶다
	~(으)ㄹ까요?	~고 있다
	~(으)ㄹ래요(?)	~기
	~(으)ㄹ 줄	~기 때문에
	~(으)러	~네요
	~(으)면	~는
	~(으)면서	~는 것
	~(으)세요	~는데
	~(으)시	~는데요
		~지만
		~지 말다
		~지 못하다
		~지 않다
		~지요

Appendix 2. Kinship Terms

1. 가족 'family'; 식구 'member of a family'

부모	parents	맏아들	first son
부모님	parents *hon.*	외아들	only son
아버지	father	딸	daughter *plain*
아버님	father *hon.*	따님	daughter *hon.*
어머니	mother	맏딸	first daughter
어머님	mother *hon.*	외딸	only daughter
할아버지	grandfather	형제	sibling(s)
할아버님	grandfather *hon.*	형	male's older brother
할머니	grandmother	형님	male's older brother *hon.*
할머님	grandmother *hon.*	누나	male's older sister
남편	husband	누님	male's older sister *hon.*
아내	wife *plain*	오빠	female's older brother
부인	wife *hon.*	언니	female's older sister
아들	son *plain*	남동생	younger brother
아드님	son *hon.*	여동생	younger sister
		막내	youngest child

2. 친척 'relative(s)'

아저씨	uncle
아주머니	aunt
큰아버지	uncle (who is one's father's older brother)
큰어머니	aunt (who is the wife of one's father's older brother)
작은아버지	uncle (who is one's father's younger brother)
작은어머니	aunt (who is the wife of one's father's younger brother)
삼촌	uncle (who is one's father's younger brother)
숙모	aunt (who is the wife of one's father's younger brother)
외삼촌	uncle (who is one's mother's brother)
외숙모	aunt (who is the wife of one's mother's brother)
고모	aunt (who is one's father's sister)
이모	aunt (who is one's mother's sister)
사촌	cousin

Appendix 3. Numbers

Arabic numeral	Sino-Korean	Native Korean	Native Korean before counters
0	영 or 공	-	-
1	일	하나	한
2	이	둘	두
3	삼	셋	세
4	사	넷	네
5	오	다섯	다섯
6	육	여섯	여섯
7	칠	일곱	일곱
8	팔	여덟	여덟
9	구	아홉	아홉
10	십	열	열
11	십일	열하나	열한
12	십이	열둘	열두
13	십삼	열셋	열세
14	십사	열넷	열네
15	십오	열다섯	열다섯
16	십육 [심뉵]	열여섯	열여섯
17	십칠	열일곱	열일곱
18	십팔	열여덟	열여덟
19	십구	열아홉	열아홉
20	이십	스물	스무
30	삼십	서른	서른
40	사십	마흔	마흔
50	오십	쉰	쉰
60	육십	예순	예순
70	칠십	일흔	일흔
80	팔십	여든	여든
90	구십	아흔	아흔
100	백		
1,000	천		
10,000	만		

Large Numbers

100	백	200	이백
1,000	천	2,000	이천
10,000	만	20,000	이만
100,000	십만	200,000	이십만
1,000,000	백만	2,000,000	이백만
10,000,000	천만	20,000,000	이천만
100,000,000	억	200,000,000	이억
1,000,000,000	십억	2,000,000,000	이십억
10,000,000,000	백억	20,000,000,000	이백억
100,000,000,000	천억	200,000,000,000	이천억
1,000,000,000,000	조	2,000,000,000,000	이조

Appendix 4. Counters

A. With Sino-Korean Numbers

Counters	What is being counted					
	층	분	과	년	월	일
	Floors of a building	Minutes	Lessons (in order)	Years	Months	Days
1	일 층	일 분	일 과	일 년	일 월	일 일
2	이 층	이 분	이 과	이 년	이 월	이 일
3	삼 층	삼 분	삼 과	삼 년	삼 월	삼 일
4	사 층	사 분	사 과	사 년	사 월	사 일
5	오 층	오 분	오 과	오 년	오 월	오 일
6	육 층	육 분	육 과	육 년	유 월	육 일
10	십 층	십 분	십 과	십 년	시 월	십 일
12	십이 층	십이 분	십이 과	십이 년	십이 월	십이 일

Counters	What is being counted					
	달러(불)	원	마일	학년	번	주일
	Dollars	Won (Korean currency)	Miles	School years	Numbers (serial)	Weeks
1	일 달러	일 원	일 마일	일학년	일 번	일 주일
2	이 달러	이 원	이 마일	이학년	이 번	이 주일
3	삼 달러	삼 원	삼 마일	삼학년	삼 번	삼 주일
4	사 달러	사 원	사 마일	사학년	사 번	사 주일
5	오 달러	오 원	오 마일	오학년	오 번	오 주일
6	육 달러	육 원	육 마일	육학년	육 번	육 주일
10	십 달러	십 원	십 마일	십학년	십 번	십 주일
12	십이 달러	십이 원	십이 마일	십이학년	십이 번	십이 주일

B. With Native Korean Numbers

Counters	What is being counted							
	명	분	시	시간	달	마리	살	과목
	People	People (hon.)	Point of time: 'the hour'	Duration: 'hours'	Duration: 'months'	Animals	Age: 'years old'	Academic subjects
1	한 명	한 분	한 시	한 시간	한 달	한 마리	한 살	한 과목
2	두 명	두 분	두 시	두 시간	두 달	두 마리	두 살	두 과목
3	세 명	세 분	세 시	세 시간	세 달	세 마리	세 살	세 과목
4	네 명	네 분	네 시	네 시간	네 달	네 마리	네 살	네 과목
5	다섯 명	다섯 분	다섯 시	다섯 시간	다섯 달	다섯 마리	다섯 살	다섯 과목
6	여섯 명	여섯 분	여섯 시	여섯 시간	여섯 달	여섯 마리	여섯 살	여섯 과목
10	열 명	열 분	열 시	열 시간	열 달	열 마리	열 살	열 과목

Counters	What is being counted							
	과	개	권	장	병	잔	번	대
	Number of lessons	Items	Volumes	Sheets (of paper)	Bottles	Cups and glasses	Times	Vehicles, cars
1	한 과	한 개	한 권	한 장	한 병	한 잔	한 번	한 대
2	두 과	두 개	두 권	두 장	두 병	두 잔	두 번	두 대
3	세 과	세 개	세 권	세 장	세 병	세 잔	세 번	세 대
4	네 과	네 개	네 권	네 장	네 병	네 잔	네 번	네 대
5	다섯 과	다섯 개	다섯 권	다섯 장	다섯 병	다섯 잔	다섯 번	다섯 대
6	여섯 과	여섯 개	여섯 권	여섯 장	여섯 병	여섯 잔	여섯 번	여섯 대
10	열 과	열 과	열 권	열 장	열 병	열 잔	열 번	열 대

Grammar Index

Item	Meaning	Lesson	
~게	adverbial suffix	L14C2	G14.3
~겠	may, will (conjecture)	L12C1	G12.2
~겠	would (intention)	L13C2	G13.5
~고	'and' (clausal connective)	L7C2	G7.3
~고 나서	after	L15C2	G15.5
~고 있다	am/are/is ~ing (progressive)	L11C1	G11.1
~고 싶다	'want to . . .' expressing desire	L10C1	G10.2
그	demonstrative expression: 'that'	L8C1	G8.2
~기	nominalizer	L16C1	G16.2
~기 때문에	because	L16C1	G16.3
~네요	indicating the speaker's reaction	L12C2	G12.3
~는	noun modifying form	L10C2	G10.5
~는 것	(an acting of) ~ing	L17C1	G17.1
~는데	clausal connective	L10C1	G10.1
~는데요	background information	L10C1	G10.3
도	comparing items: 'also, too'	L1C1	G1.3
못	negative adverb: 'cannot'	L6C2	G6.4
무슨	'what (kind of) N'	L7C1	G7.2
~습니다/ㅂ니다	deferential ending for a statement	L8C2	G8.3
~습니까/ㅂ니까?	deferential ending for a question	L8C2	G8.3
아니에요	'to not be' (identification)	L1C2	G1.5
안	negative adverb: 'do not'	L6C2	G6.4
어느	'which N'	L7C1	G7.2
~어/아 보다	'try doing'	L16C1	G16.1
~어/아 주다	benefactive expression	L13C1	G13.1
~어/아 드리다	benefactive expression	L16C2	G16.4
~어/아야 되다	expressing obligation or necessity	L13C1	G13.2
~어서/아서	clausal connective: cause	L10C2	G10.4
~어서/아서	clausal connective: sequential	L12C1	G12.1
~어요/아요	polite ending	L2C2	G2.5
~었/았/ㅆ어요	past tense	L6C2	G6.3

L = lesson, C = conversation, G = grammar

Item	Meaning	Lesson	
에	'in, at, on' (static location)	L2C1	G2.2
에	'to' (destination)	L5C1	G5.1
에서	'in, at' (dynamic location)	L5C1	G5.1
~(으)ㄴ	noun modifying form	L9C1	G9.2
~(으)ㄴ	noun modifying form (past)	L12C2	G12.5
~(으)ㄴ데	clausal connective	L10C1	G10.1
~(으)ㄴ데요	background information	L10C1	G10.3
~(으)ㄹ	noun modifying form (prospective)	L15C2	G15.4
~(으)ㄹ 거예요	probability suffix	L7C1	G7.1
~(으)ㄹ 때	'when'	L17C2	G17.4
~(으)ㄹ 수	can/cannot	L15C1	G15.1
~(으)ㄹ 줄	'how to'	L17C2	G17.5
~(으)ㄹ까요?	'Shall I/we?; Do you think?'	L11C2	G11.4
~(으)ㄹ게요	'I will' (promise)	L13C1	G13.3
~(으)ㄹ래요(?)	'Would you like to..? I would like to...'	L11C1	G11.2
~(으)러	'in order to'	L5C2	G5.3
(으)로	'by means of'	L6C1	G6.1
(으)로	'toward, to'	L8C2	G8.4
~(으)면	'if . . .'	L17C1	G17.2
~(으)면서	'while ~ing'	L15C2	G15.3
~(으)세요	honorific polite ending	L3C1	G3.2
~(으)시	subject honorifics	L9C2	G9.4
은/는	topic particle: 'as for'	L1C1	G1.1
은/는	comparing items	L1C1	G1.3
은/는	changing topics	L2C1	G2.3
을/를	object particle	L3C2	G3.3
이	demonstrative expression: 'this'	L8C1	G8.2
이/가	subject particle	L2C1	G2.1
~(이)나	as much/many as	L11C2	G11.3
이에요/예요	'to be' (equation)	L1C1	G1.1
저	demonstrative: 'that (over there)'	L8C1	G8.2
~지 말다/마세요	to stop, cease	L14C2	G14.4
~지 못하다	cannot	L14C1	G14.2
~지 않다	to not be, to not do	L16C2	G16.5
~지만	'but, although'	L9C2	G9.5
~지요	'. . . isn't it?' (seeking agreement)	L8C1	G8.1

Korean - English Glossary

1학년	freshman
2학년	sophomore
3학년	junior
4학년	senior
가	subject particle
가게	store
가깝다	to be close, near
가끔	sometimes
가다	to go
가르치다	to teach
가방	bag
가수	singer
가운데	the middle, the center
가위, 바위, 보	rock-paper-scissors
가을	autumn, fall
가장	the most
가족	family
갈비	*kalbi* (barbecued spareribs)
갈아 입다	to change (clothes)
갈아 타다	to change (vehicles)
감기에 걸리다	to have, catch a cold
감사하다	to be thankful
값	price
갖고 가다	to take
갖고 다니다	to carry around
갖고 오다	to bring
갖다 놓다	to bring and put down somewhere
갖다 드리다*hum*	to bring/take something to someone
갖다 주다	to bring/take something to someone
같이	together
개1	dog
개2	item (counter)
거	thing (contraction of 것)
거기	there
거리1	distance
거리2	street
건강하다	to be healthy
건너다	to cross
건너편	the other side
건물	building
건축학	architecture
걷다	to walk
걸리다	to take [time]
걸어가다	to go on foot
걸어다니다	to walk around
걸어오다	to come on foot
것	thing (=거)
게임	game
겨울	winter
결혼	marriage
결혼하다	to get married
경기	match, game
경제학	economics
계단	stairs
계산서	check
계시다*hon.*	to be (existence), stay
계절	season
계획	plan
계획하다	to plan
고등학교	high school
고등학생	high school student
고르다	to choose, select
고맙다	to be thankful
고장	breakdown
고추장	red-pepper paste
고향	hometown
골프	golf
곳	place
공	0 (zero: for phone #)
공부	study
공부하다	to study
공원	park
공포 영화	horror movie
공항	airport
과1	lesson, chapter
과2	and (joins nouns) (narration only)
과목	course, subject
과일	fruit
과자	cracker
괜찮다	to be all right, okay
굉장히	very much

교과서	textbook
교수님	professor
교실	classroom
교육학	education
교통	traffic
교회	church
구경하다	to look around; to sightsee
구두 시험	oral exam
귀걸이	earring
군데	place, spot
권	volume (counter)
그	that
그냥	just, without any special reason
그동안	meantime
그래서	so, therefore
그런데	1. but, however; 2. by the way
그럼	(if so) then
그렇다	to be so
그렇지만	but, however
그리고	and
그리다	to draw
그림	picture, painting
그만	without doing anything further
극장	movie theater
근처	nearby, vicinity
글쎄요	Well; It's hard to say
금반지	gold ring
금방	soon
금요일	Friday
기계 공학	mechanical engineering
기다리다	to wait
기분	feeling
기사	driver
기숙사	dormitory
기차	train
기타	guitar
길	street, road
길다	to be long
김밥	*kimpab*
김치	*kimchi*
까만색	black(=까망)
까맣다	to be black

까지	1. up to (location); 2. to/until/through (time); 3. including
깨끗하다	to be clean
께*hon.*	to (a person)
께서*hon.*	subject particle (=이/가*plain*)
꽃	flower
꽃집	flower shop
꿈(을) 꾸다	to dream a dream
끝나다	to be over, finished
끼다	to wear (glasses, gloves, rings)
나*plain*	I (=저*hum.*)
나가다	to go out
나다	happen, break out
나라	country
나쁘다	to be bad
나오다	to come out
나이	age
나중에	later
날	day
날마다	every day
날씨	weather
남기다	to leave (a message)
남동생	younger brother
남자	man
내*plain*	my (=제*hum.*)
내년	next year
(돈을)내다	to pay
내려가다	to go down
내리다	to get off
내일	tomorrow
냉면	*naengmyŏn* (cold buckwheat noodles)
너	you
너무	too much
넓다	to be spacious, wide
네	1. yes; 2. I see; 3. okay
년	year (counter)
노랗다	to be yellow
노래	song
노래 부르다	to sing
노래방	karaoke room

녹차	green tea	데이트(하다)	to date
놀다	to play; to not work	도	also, too
농구	basketball	도서관	library
농구 시합	basketball game	도시	city
놓아 주다	to put something down for someone	도착하다	to arrive
		도쿄	Tokyo
누가	who (누구 + 가)	독서	reading
누구	who	돈	money
누나	the older sister of a male	돈이 들다	to cost money
		돈을 내다	to pay
눈1	eyes	돈을 벌다	to earn money
눈2	snow	돌	the first birthday
눈(이) 오다	to snow	돌다	to turn
뉴스	news	돌려 드리다*hum.*	to return (something to someone)
뉴욕	New York		
는	topic particle ('as for')	돌려 주다	to return (something to someone)
늦게	late		
늦다	to be late	돌아가시다*hon.*	to pass away
늦잠	oversleep	돌아오다	to return, come back
다	all	돕다	to help
다니다	to attend	동네	neighborhood
다르다	to be different	동대문시장	East Gate Market
다시	again	동부	East Coast
다음	next, following	동생	younger sibling
다음부터(는)	from next time	동안	during
달	month (counter)	동양학	Asian studies
달다	to be sweet	되다	to become, get, turn into
달러	dollar (=불)		
닮다	to resemble	된장찌개	soybean-paste stew
담배	cigarette	두	two (with counter)
답	answer	두 번째	the second
대답	answer	둘	two
대답하다	to answer	뒤	the back, behind
대통령	president	드라마	drama
대통령 선거	presidential election	드럼	drum
대학	college, university	드리다*hum.*	to give (=주다*plain*)
대학교	college, university	드시다*hon.*	to eat (=먹다*plain*)
대학생	college student	듣다	1. to listen;
대학원	graduate school		2. to take a course
대학원생	graduate student	들	plural particle
댁*hon.*	home, house (=집*plain*)	들어가다	to enter
더	more	들어오다	to come in
더럽다	to be dirty	등	et cetera
덜	less	등산	hiking
덥다	to be hot	등산하다	to hike
덮다	to close, cover	따님*hon.*	daughter
데	place	따뜻하다	to be warm

따라하다	to repeat after	머리	1. head;
딸	daughter		2. hair
때	time	먹다	to eat
때문에	because of	멀다	to be far
또	and, also, too	메뉴	menu
똑바로	straight, upright	메시지	message
뛰다	to run	멕시코	Mexico
뜨겁다	to be hot	며칠	what date; a few
뜻하다	to mean, signify		days
라디오	radio	명	people (counter)
라면	instant noodles	몇	how many, what (with
	(ramen)		a counter)
라운지	lounge	모두	all
랩	lab	모레	the day after
러시아	Russia		tomorrow
로스앤젤레스	Los Angeles (L.A.)	모르다	to not know, be
록	rock music		unaware of
룸메이트	roommate	모으다	to collect
를	object particle	모자	cap, hat
마리	animal (counter)	목(이) 마르다	to be thirsty
마시다	to drink	목걸이	necklace
마중 나가다	to go out to greet	목소리	voice
	someone	목요일	Thursday
마중 나오다	to come out to greet	목욕	bath
	someone	목욕하다	to bathe
마켓	market	몸	body
막내	youngest child	몸조리	care of health
막히다	to be blocked,	못	cannot
	congested	무섭다	to be scary; scared
만	only	무슨	what, what kind of
만나다	to meet	무엇	what (=뭐)
만들다	to make	무척	very much
만화책	comic book	문	door
많다	to be many, much	문학	literature
많이	much, many	문화	culture
말	speech, words	묻다	to ask
말씀 *hon.*	speech, words	물	water
	(=말 *plain*)	물가	cost of living
말하다	to speak	물건	merchandise
맛없다	to be tasteless, not	물리학	physics
	delicious	물어보다	to inquire
맛있다	to be delicious	뭐	what (=무엇)
매년	every year	미국	the United States
매달	every month	미안하다	to be sorry
매일	every day	밑	the bottom, below
매주	every week	바꾸다	to change, switch
맵다	to be spicy	바닷가	beach

바쁘다	to be busy	볼링	bowling
바이올린	violin	볼펜	ballpoint pen
바지	pants	봄	spring
박스	box	뵙다 *hum.*	to see (=보다 *plain*)
밖	outside	부르다 (노래)	to sing (a song)
밖에	nothing but, only	부모님	parents
반	half	부엌	kitchen
반1	class	부자	a wealthy person
반2	half	부치다	to mail (a letter, parcel)
반갑다	to be glad		
반지	ring	부탁하다	to ask a favor
반찬	side dishes	부터	from (time) . . .
받다	to receive	분	minute (counter)
발	foot	분 *hon.*	people (=명 *plain*)
밤	night	불	dollar (=달러)
밥	1. cooked rice; 2. meal	불고기	*pulgogi* (roast meat)
		불편하다	to be uncomfortable, inconvenient
방	room		
방학	school vacation	브로드웨이 극장	Broadway theater
배	stomach, abdomen		
배(가) 고프다	to be hungry	비	rain
배(가) 부르다	to have a full stomach	비(가) 오다	to rain
배우다	to learn	비빔밥	*pibimpap* (rice with vegetables and beef)
백만	million		
백화점	department store	비싸다	to be expensive
밴쿠버	Vancouver	비행기	airplane
버스	bus	빌딩	building
번	1. number (counter); 2. number of times (e.g., 한 번)	빌려주다	to lend
		빌리다	to borrow
		빠르다	to be fast
번째	ordinal numbers	빨갛다	to be red
번호	number	빨래하다	to do the laundry
벌다	to earn (money)	빨리	fast, quickly
벌써	already	사	4
법학	law	사거리	intersection
벗다	to take off, undress	사고	accident
별로	not really/particularly	사귀다	to make friends
보내다1	to spend time	사다	to buy
보내다2	to send	사람	person, people
보다	than	사랑하다	to love
보다	to see, look, watch	사모님	teacher's wife
보스톤	Boston	사이	1. relationship; 2. between
보이다	to be seen, visible		
보통	usually	사이즈	size
복	good fortune	사전	dictionary
복습	review	사진	photo, picture
복잡하다	to be crowded	살	years old

살다	to live	쉬다	to rest
삼	3	쉽다	to be easy
상	table	슈퍼	supermarket
새	new	스릴러	thriller
새로	newly	스웨터	sweater
새벽	dawn	스키	ski
새해	New Year	스키 타다	to ski
색	color (=색깔)	스트레스	stress
샌드위치	sandwich	스파게티	spaghetti
생물학	biology	스페인	Spain
생신hon.	birthday	스포츠	sports
생일	birthday	슬프다	to be sad
생활	daily life, living	시1	hour, o'clock
샤워	shower	시간	time, hour (duration)
샤워하다	to take a shower	시계	clock, watch
서로	each other	시끄럽다	to be noisy
서비스	service	시다	to be sour
서울	Seoul	시드니	Sydney
서점	bookstore (=책방)	시원하다	to be cool, refreshing
선물	present, gift	시작하다	to begin
선물하다	to give a present, gift	시장	marketplace
선생님	teacher	시청	city hall
설거지	dishwashing	시청역	city hall station
설거지하다	to wash dishes	시카고	Chicago
설악산	Seol-ak Mount	시키다	to order (food)
성격	personality	시험	test, exam
성함hon.	name (=이름plain)	식당	restaurant
세수하다	to wash one's face	식사	meal
세일	sale	식사하다	to have a meal
센트	cent	신나다	to be excited
셔츠	shirt	신다	to wear (footwear)
소설	novel	신문	newspaper
손(을) 씻다	to wash one's hands	신발	shoes
손님	guest, customer	신호등	traffic light
쇼핑	shopping	실	thread
쇼핑하다	to shop	실례하다	to be excused
수고하다	to put forth effort, take trouble	싫다	to be undesirable
		싫어하다	to dislike
수도	capital (city)	심리학	psychology
수업	course, class	심심하다	to be bored
수영	swimming	싱겁다	to be bland
수영장	swimming pool	싶다	to want to
수영하다	to swim	싸다	to be cheap
수요일	Wednesday	쓰다	1. to write;
숙제	homework		2. to use;
숙제하다	to do homework		3. to wear headgear;
순두부찌개	soft tofu stew		4. to be bitter

씨	attached to a person's name for courtesy	어리다	to be young
아	oh	어머	Oh! Oh my! Dear me!
아니다	to not be (negative equation)	어머니	mother
		어서	quick(ly)
아니요	no	어제	yesterday
아들	son	어젯밤	last night
아마	probably, perhaps	언니	the older sister of a female
아버지	father	언어학	linguistics
아이	child	언제	when
아이스하키	ice hockey	얼굴	face
아저씨	mister; a man of one's parents' age	얼마	how long/much
		얼마나	how long/much
아주	very, really	엄마	mom
아직	yet, still	없다	1. to not be (existence);
아침	1. breakfast;		2. to not have
	2. morning	에	1. in, at, on (static location);
아파트	apartment		2. to (destination);
아프다	to be sick		3. at, in, on (time);
악기	musical instrument		4. for, per
안1	the inside	에서	1. in, at (dynamic location);
안2	do not		2. from (location);
안경	eyeglasses		3. from (time)
안녕하다	to be well	엘리베이터	elevator
안녕히	in peace	여기	here
안부	regards	여동생	younger sister
앉다	to sit	여러	many, several
않다	to not to be, to not do	여름	summer
알다	to know	여보	honey, dear
알아보다	to find out, check out	여보세요	hello (on the phone)
앞	the front	여자	woman
액션	action	여자 친구	girlfriend
야구	baseball	여행	travel
약국	drugstore	여행하다	to travel
약속	1. engagement;	역	station
	2. promise	역사	history
양말	socks, stockings	연구실	professor's office
양식	Western-style (food)	연극	play
애기	talk, chat (=이야기)	연락	contact
애기하다	to talk, chat	연세 *hon.*	age
어	oh	연습	practice
어느	which	연습하다	to practice
어디	what place, where	연주	musical performance
어떤	which, what kind of	연주	to perform on a musical instrument
어떻게	how		
어떻다	to be how		
어렵다	to be difficult		

연필	pencil	웬일	what matter
열다	to open	위	the top side, above
열심히	diligently	유니온 빌딩	Union Building
영	0 (zero)	육개장	hot shredded beef
영국	the United Kingdom		soup
영어	the English language	으로1	by means of
영화	movie	으로2	toward, to
옆	the side, beside	은	topic particle ('as for')
예	yes, I see, okay (=네)	은행	bank
예쁘다	to be pretty	을	object particle
오늘	today	음료수	beverage
오다	to come	음식	food
오래	long time	음식점	restaurant (=식당)
오래간만	after a long time	음악	music
오른쪽	right side	음악회	concert
오빠	the older brother of a	의	of
	female	의사	doctor
오전	a.m.	의자	chair
오후	afternoon	이1	2
올라가다	to go up	이2	subject particle
올림	Sincerely yours.	이3	this
올림픽	Olympic	이4	a suffix inserted after
올해	this year		a Korean first name
옷	clothes		that ends in a
옷가게	clothing store		consonant
와	and (joins nouns)	이5	tooth
	(narration only)	이거	this (=이것)
왜	why	이기다	to win
외식하다	to eat out	이다	to be (equation)
왼쪽	left side	이(를) 닦다	to brush one's teeth
요리	cooking	이따가	a little later
요리하다	to cook	이름	name
요즘	these days	이메일	e-mail
우리 plain	we/us/our (=저희 hum.)	이번	this time
우산	umbrella	이사하다	to move
우체국	post office	이스트 홀	East Hall
우표	stamp	이야기	talk, chat (=애기)
운동	exercise	이야기하다	to talk (=애기하다)
운동장	playground	이젠	now (이제+는)
운동하다	to exercise	이쪽으로	this way + 으로
운동화	sports shoes, sneakers	이태리	Italy
운전하다	to drive	인구	population
원 (₩)	won (Korean	인사	greeting
	currency)	인사하다	to greet
월	month (counter)	인천	Incheon
월드컵	World Cup	인터넷	Internet
월요일	Monday	인터뷰	interview

일1	1
일2	day (counter)
일3	work
일4	event
일 인 분	one portion
일본	Japan
일식	Japanese-style (food)
일어나다	to get up
일요일	Sunday
일찍	early
일하다	to work
읽다	to read
입구	entrance
입다	to wear, put on (clothes)
있다	1. to be (existence); 2. to have
자다	to sleep
자라다	to grow up
자르다	to cut
자리	seat
자전거	bicycle
자주	often, frequently
작년	last year
작다	to be small (in size)
잔	glass, cup
잔치	feast, party
잘	well
잘라 드리다 *hum.*	to cut (something for someone)
잘라 주다	to cut (something for someone)
잠	sleep
잠깐만	for a short time
잡다	to catch, grab
잡지	magazine
장(을) 보다	to buy one's groceries
장갑	gloves
재미없다	to be uninteresting
재미있다	to be interesting, fun
재즈	jazz
저	that (over there)
저 *hum.*	I (=나 *plain*)
저기	over there
저녁	1. evening; 2. dinner
저어	uh (expression of hesitation)
저희 *hum.*	we/us/our (=우리 *plain*)
적다	to be few, scarce
적어도	at least
전	before
전공	major
전공하다	to major
전기공학	electrical engineering
전부	all together
전화	telephone
전화 번호	telephone number
전화비	telephone bill
전화하다	to make a telephone call
점심	lunch
점원	clerk, salesperson
정류장	(bus) stop
정말	really
정치학	political science
제 *hum.*	my (=내 *plain*)
제일	first, most
조금	a little (=좀)
조심하다	to be careful
조용하다	to be quiet
졸다	to doze off
졸업(하다)	graduation
좀	a little (contraction of 조금)
좁다	to be narrow
종업원	employee
좋다	to be good, nice
좋아하다	to like
죄송하다	to be sorry
주	week
주다	to give
주말	weekend
주무시다 *hon.*	to sleep (=자다 *plain*)
주문하다	to order
주소	address
주스	juice
주인공	main character
죽다	to die
준비	preparation
준비하다	to prepare
중국	China

중식	Chinese-style (food)	취미	hobby
중에서	between, among	층	floor, layer (counter)
중학교	middle school	치다	1. to play (tennis)
중학생	middle school student		2. to play (piano,
즐겁다	to be joyful		guitar)
지금	now	치마	skirt
지난	last, past	친구	friend
지내다	to get along	친절하다	to be kind, considerate
지다	to lose	칠판	blackboard
지도	map	카드	card
지하철	subway	캐나다	Canada
직접	directly	캠퍼스	campus
질문	question	커피	coffee
집	home, house	커피숍	coffee shop, café
짜다	to be salty	컴퓨터	computer
짧다	to be short	컴퓨터 랩	computer lab
째	ordinal numbers	케이크	cake
쪽	side, direction	켜다	to play (violin)
쭉	straight	켤레	pair
쯤	about, around	코미디	comedy
찍다	to take (a photo)	쿠바	Cuba
차	tea	크게	loud(ly)
차	car	크다	to be big
차다	to be cold	크리스마스	Christmas
차비	fare (bus, taxi)	큰아버지	uncle (father's older
착하다	to be good-natured,		brother)
	kind-hearted	클래스	class
참	1. really, truly;	클래식	classical music
	2. by the way	클럽	club
찾다	to find, look for	키	height
책	book	키가 작다	to be short
책방	bookstore	키가 크다	to be tall
책상	desk	타고 가다	to go riding
처음	the first time	타고 다니다	to come/go riding
천천히	slow(ly)	타고 오다	to come riding
첫	first	타다	to get in/on, ride
청바지	blue jeans	타이레놀	tylenol
청소	cleaning	태권도	Korean martial art
청소하다	to clean	태어나다	to be born
초등학교	elementary school	택시	taxi
초등학생	elementary school	택시비	taxi fare
	student	테니스	tennis
축구	soccer	테니스장	tennis court
축하하다	to congratulate	텔레비전	television
출구	exit	토요일	Saturday
춤추다	to dance	통화	phone call
춥다	to be cold	트럭	truck

특히	particularly
틀다	to turn on, switch on, play (music)
파랗다	to be blue
파티	party
팔다	to sell
펜	pen
펴다	to open, unfold
편리하다	to be convenient
편지	letter
편하다	to be comfortable, convenient
풋볼	football
프랑스	France
피곤하다	to be tired
피아노	piano
피우다	to smoke
피자	pizza
하고	1. and (with nouns); 2. with
하나	one
하다	to do
하루	(one) day
하얗다	to be white
하와이	Hawai'i
학교	school
학기	semester, academic term
학년	school year
학비	tuition fees
학생	student
학생회관	student center
한	one (with counter)
한국	Korea

한국말	the Korean language
한국어	the Korean language
한국학	Korean Studies
한글	Korean alphabet
한복	traditional Korean dress
한식	Korean-style (food)
한인타운	Korea town
한테	to (a person or an animal)
한테서	from (a person or an animal)
할머니	grandmother
할아버지	grandfather
햄버거	hamburger
행복하다	to be happy
헤드폰	headphones
형	the older brother of a male
형님 *hon.*	the older brother of a male
형제	sibling(s)
호선	subway line
호주	Australia
홍콩	Hong Kong
화요일	Tuesday
화장실	bathroom, restroom
후	after
휴게실	lounge
휴일	holiday, day off
흐리다	to be cloudy
힘(이) 들다	to be hard

English - Korean Glossary

0 (zero)	공; 영
1	일
2	이
3	삼
4	사
about	쯤
above	위
academic term	학기
accident	사고
action	액션
address	주소
after	후
after a long time	오래간만
afternoon	오후
again	다시
age	나이; 연세hon.
airplane	비행기
airport	공항
a little	조금 (= 좀)
a little	좀 (= 조금)
a little later	이따가
all	다; 모두
all right [to be]	괜찮다
all together	전부
already	벌써
also	또
also (particle)	도
a.m.	오전
among	중에서
and	그리고
and	또
and	와/과 (with nouns)
and	하고 (with nouns)
animal	마리 (counter)
answer	답; 대답
apartment	아파트
architecture	건축학
around	쯤
arrive [to]	도착하다
Asian studies	동양학
ask [to]	묻다
ask a favor [to]	부탁하다
at	에서 (dynamic location)
at	에 (static location)
at	에 (time)
at least	적어도
attached to a person's name for courtesy	씨
attend [to]	다니다
Australia	호주
autumn	가을
back [the]	뒤
bad [to be]	나쁘다
bag	가방
ballpoint pen	볼펜
bank	은행
barbecued spareribs	갈비
baseball	야구
basketball	농구
basketball game	농구 시합
bath	목욕
bathe [to]	목욕하다
bathroom	화장실
be [to]	이다 (equation)
be [to]	없다 (existence)
be [to]	계시다hon. (existence)
be [to]	있다 (existence)
be [to not]	아니다 (negative equation)
be [to not]	~지 않다
be so [to]	그렇다
beach	바닷가
because of	때문에
become [to]	되다
before	전
begin [to]	시작하다
behind	뒤
below	밑, 아래
beside	옆
between	사이
between	중에서
beverage	음료수
bicycle	자전거
big [to be]	크다
biology	생물학
birthday	생일; 생신hon.
bitter [to be]	쓰다

black [to be]	까맣다	catch a cold [to]	감기에 걸리다
blackboard	칠판	cent	센트
black color	까만색 (=까망)	center [the]	가운데
bland [to be]	싱겁다	chair	의자
blocked [to be]	막히다	change [to]	갈아 입다 (clothes)
blue [to be]	파랗다	change [to]	갈아 타다
blue jeans	청바지		(vehicles)
body	몸	change [to]	바꾸다
book	책	chapter	과
bookstore	책방, 서점	chat	이야기(=얘기)
bored [to be]	심심하다	chat [to]	얘기하다,
born [to be]	태어나다		이야기하다
borrow [to]	빌리다	cheap [to be]	싸다
Boston	보스톤	check	계산서
bottom [the]	밑, 아래	check out [to]	알아보다
bowling	볼링	Chicago	시카고
box	박스	child	아이
breakdown	고장	China	중국
breakfast	아침	Chinese style	중식 (food)
bring [to]	갖고 오다	choose [to]	고르다
bring and put	갖다 놓다	Christmas	크리스마스
down [to]		church	교회
Broadway theater	브로드웨이 극장	cigarette	담배
brush one's	이(를) 닦다	city	도시
teeth [to]		city hall	시청
building	건물, 빌딩	city hall station	시청역
bus	버스	class	반; 수업; 클래스
bus stop	정류장	classical music	클래식
busy [to be]	바쁘다	classroom	교실
but	그런데; 그렇지만	clean [to]	청소하다
buy [to]	사다	clean [to be]	깨끗하다
buy one's groceries	장(을) 보다	cleaning	청소
by means of	(으)로	clerk	점원
by the way	그런데; 참	clock	시계
café	커피숍	close [to]	덮다
cake	케이크	close [to be]	가깝다
campus	캠퍼스	clothes	옷
Canada	캐나다	clothing store	옷가게
cannot	못	cloudy [to be]	흐리다
cap	모자	club	클럽
capital (city)	수도	coffee	커피
car	차	coffee shop	커피숍
card	카드	cold [to be]	차다; 춥다
careful [to be]	조심하다	cold noodle dish	냉면
care of health	몸조리	collect [to]	모으다
carry around	갖고 다니다	college	대학, 대학교
catch [to]	잡다	college student	대학생

color	색 (=색깔)	day	일 (counter)
come [to]	오다	day after tomorrow	모레
come back [to]	돌아오다	day off	휴일
comedy	코미디	dear (spouse)	여보
come in [to]	들어오다	Dear me!	어머
come on foot	걸어오다	delicious [to be]	맛있다
come out [to]	나오다	delicious [to be not]	맛없다
come out to greet	마중 나오다	department store	백화점
someone [to]		desk	책상
come riding [to]	타고 오다	dictionary	사전
comfortable	편하다	die [to]	죽다
comic book	만화책	different [to be]	다르다
computer	컴퓨터	difficult [to be]	어렵다
computer lab	컴퓨터 랩	diligently	열심히
concert	음악회	dinner	저녁
congested [to be]	막히다	direction	쪽
congratulate [to]	축하하다	directly	직접
considerate [to be]	친절하다	dirty [to be]	더럽다
contact	연락	dishwashing	설거지
contact [to]	연락하다	dislike [to]	싫어하다
convenient [to be]	편리하다; 편하다	distance	거리
cook [to]	요리하다	do [to]	하다
cooked rice	밥	do [to not]	~지 않다
cooking	요리	doctor	의사
cool [to]	시원하다	dog	개
cost money [to]	돈이 들다	dollar	불 (=달러)
cost of living	물가	do not	안
country	나라	door	문
course	과목; 수업	dormitory	기숙사
cover [to]	덮다	doze off [to]	졸다
cracker	과자	drama	드라마
cross [to]	건너다	draw [to]	그리다
crowded [to be]	복잡하다	dream a dream	꿈(을) 꾸다
Cuba	쿠바	drink [to]	마시다
culture	문화	drive [to]	운전하다
cup	잔	driver	기사
customer	손님	drugstore	약국
cut [to]	자르다	drum	드럼
cut something	잘라 드리다hon.	during	동안
(for someone) [to]		each other	서로
cut something	잘라 주다	early	일찍
(for someone) [to]		earn [to]	벌다
dance [to]	춤추다	earn money [to]	돈을 벌다
date [to]	데이트(하다)	earring	귀걸이
daughter	딸; 따님hon.	East Coast	동부
dawn	새벽	East Gate market	동대문 시장
day	날	East Hall	이스트 홀

easy [to be]	쉽다	first	제일; 첫
eat [to]	먹다; 드시다*hon.*	first birthday	돌
eat out [to]	외식하다	first time	처음
economics	경제학	floor	층 (counter)
education	교육학	flower	꽃
electrical	전기공학	flower shop	꽃집
engineering		following	다음
elementary school	초등학교	food	음식
elementary school	초등학생	foot	발
student		football	풋볼
elevator	엘리베이터	for	에
e-mail	이메일	for a short time	잠깐만
employee	종업원	France	프랑스
engagement	약속	frequently	자주
English language	영어	freshman	1학년
enter [to]	들어가다	Friday	금요일
entrance	입구	friend	친구
et cetera	등	from	한테서 (a person
evening	저녁		or an animal)
event	일	from	에서 (location)
every day	날마다; 매일	from	부터 (time)
every month	매달	from next time	다음부터(는)
every week	매주	front	앞
every year	매년	fruit	과일
exam	시험	fun [to be]	재미있다
excited [to be]	신나다	game	게임; 경기(match)
excused [to be]	실례하다	get [to]	되다
exercise	운동	get along [to]	지내다
exercise [to]	운동하다	get in [to]	타다
exit	출구	get off [to]	내리다
expensive [to be]	비싸다	get on [to]	타다
eyeglasses	안경	get up [to]	일어나다
eyes	눈	gift	선물
face	얼굴	girlfriend	여자 친구
fall	가을	give [to]	주다; 드리다*hum.*
family	가족	give a present [to]	선물하다
far [to be]	멀다	glad [to be]	반갑다
fare	차비 (bus, taxi)	glass	잔
fast	빨리	gloves	장갑
fast [to be]	빠르다	go [to]	가다
father	아버지	go down [to]	내려가다
feast	잔치	gold ring	금반지
feeling	기분	golf	골프
few [to be]	적다	good [to be]	좋다
find [to]	찾다	good-natured [to be]	착하다
find out [to]	알아보다	go on foot [to]	걸어가다
finished [to be]	끝나다	go out [to]	나가다

go out to greet someone [to]	마중 나가다	homework	숙제
		homework [to do]	숙제하다
go riding [to]	타고 가다	honey	여보
go up [to]	올라가다	Hong Kong	홍콩
grab [to]	잡다	horror movie	공포 영화
graduate [to]	졸업하다	hot [to be]	덥다; 뜨겁다
graduate school	대학원	hot shredded beef soup	육개장
graduate student	대학원생		
graduation	졸업	hour	시
grandfather	할아버지	house	집; 댁hon.
grandmother	할머니	how	어떻게
green tea	녹차	how [to be]	어떻다
greet [to]	인사하다	however	그런데; 그렇지만
greeting	인사	how long/much	얼마; 얼마나
grow up [to]	자라다	how many	몇
guest	손님	hungry [to be]	배(가) 고프다
guitar	기타	I	나; 저hum.
hair	머리	ice hockey	아이스하키
half	반	in	에서 (dynamic location)
hamburger	햄버거		
happy [to be]	행복하다	in	에 (static location)
hard [to be]	힘(이) 들다	in	에 (time)
hat	모자	Incheon	인천
have [to]	있다	including	까지
have [to not]	없다	inconvenient [to be]	불편하다
have a cold [to]	감기에 걸리다	inquire [to]	물어보다
have a full stomach [to]	배(가) 부르다	inside	안
		instant noodles	라면 (ramen)
have a meal [to]	식사하다	interesting [to be]	재미있다
Hawai'i	하와이	Internet	인터넷
head	머리	intersection	사거리
headphones	헤드폰	interview	인터뷰
healthy [to be]	건강하다	I see	네, 예
height	키	item	개 (counter)
hello	여보세요 (on the phone)	It's hard to say	글쎄요
		Italy	이태리
help [to]	돕다	Japan	일본
here	여기	Japanese-style	일식 (food)
high school	고등학교	jazz	재즈
high school student	고등학생	joyful [to be]	즐겁다
hike [to]	등산하다	juice	주스
hiking	등산	junior	3학년
history	역사	just	그냥
hobby	취미	kalbi	불고기
holiday	휴일	karaoke	노래방
home	집; 댁hon.	kid	아이
hometown	고향	kimchi	김치

kimbab	김밥	lounge	휴게실 (=라운지)
kind [to be]	친절하다	lunch	점심
kind-hearted [to be]	착하다	magazine	잡지
kitchen	부엌	mail [to]	부치다 (a letter, parcel)
know [to]	알다		
know [to not]	모르다	main character	주인공
Korea	한국	major	전공
Korea town	한인타운	major [to]	전공하다
Korean alphabet	한글	make [to]	만들다
Korean language	한국말; 한국어	make a telephone call [to]	전화하다
Korean martial art	태권도		
Korean-style (food)	한식	make friends [to]	사귀다
lab	랩	man	남자
last	지난	man of one's parents' age	아저씨
last night	어젯밤		
last year	작년	many [to be]	많이; 여러
late	늦게	many [to be]	많다
late [to be]	늦다	map	지도
later	나중에, 이따가	market	마켓
law	법학	marketplace	시장
layer	층 (counter)	marriage	결혼
learn [to]	배우다	married [to get]	결혼하다
leave [to]	남기다 (a message)	match	경기
		meal	식사; 밥
left side	왼쪽	mean [to]	뜻하다
lend [to]	빌려주다	meantime	그동안
less	덜	mechanical engineering	기계 공학
lesson	과		
letter	편지	meet [to]	만나다
library	도서관	menu	메뉴
life	생활	merchandise	물건
like [to]	좋아하다	message	메시지
linguistics	언어학	Mexico	멕시코
listen [to]	듣다	middle [the]	가운데
literature	문학	middle school	중학교
live [to]	살다	middle school student	중학생
living	생활		
long [to be]	길다	million	백만
long time	오래	minute	분 (counter)
look [to]	보다	mister	아저씨
look around [to]	구경하다	mom	엄마
look for [to]	찾다	Monday	월요일
Los Angeles	로스앤젤레스	money	돈
lose [to]	지다	month	달 (counter)
love [to]	사랑하다	month	월 (counter)
loud [to be]	크다	more	더
loud(ly)	크게	morning	아침

most	제일	okay [to be]	괜찮다
most [the]	가장	older brother of a female [the]	오빠
mother	어머니		
move [to]	이사하다	older brother of a male [the]	형
movie	영화		
movie theater	극장	older brother of a male [the]	형님 hon.
much	많이		
much [to be]	많다	older sister of a female [the]	언니
music	음악		
musical instrument	악기	older sister of a male [the]	누나
musical performance	연주		
		Olympic	올림픽
my	내; 제 hum.	on	에 (static location)
naengmyŏn	냉면	on	에 (time)
name	이름; 성함 hon.	one	하나
narrow [to be]	좁다	one	한 (with counter)
near [to be]	가깝다	one day	하루
nearby	근처	one portion	일 인 분
necklace	목걸이	only	만; 밖에
neighborhood	동네	open [to]	열다; 펴다
new	새	oral exam	구두 시험
New Year	새해	order [to]	시키다, 주문하다
newly	새로	ordinal numbers	째/번째
news	뉴스	other side [the]	건너편
newspaper	신문	our	우리; 저희 hum.
New York	뉴욕	outside	밖
next	다음	over [to be]	끝나다
next year	내년	oversleep	늦잠
nice [to be]	좋다	over there	저기
night	밤	painting	그림
no	아니요	pair	켤레
noisy [to be]	시끄럽다	pants	바지
nothing but	밖에	parents	부모님
really [(not)]	별로	park	공원
novel	소설	particularly	특히
now	지금; 이제	party	잔치; 파티
number	번호	pass away [to]	돌아가시다 hon.
number	번 (counter)	past	지난
number of times	번(e.g., 한 번)	pay [to]	돈을 내다
object particle	을, 를	peace [in]	안녕히
occasionally	자주	pen	펜
o'clock	시	pencil	연필
of	의	people	사람
often	자주	people	명; 분 hon.(counter)
oh! Oh my! Dear me!	아; 어; 어머	per	에
		perhaps	아마
okay/OK	네 (=예)	person	사람

personality	성격	rain	비
phone call	통화	rain [to]	비(가) 오다
photo	사진	read [to]	읽다
physics	물리학	reading	독서
piano	피아노	really	아주; 정말; 참
pibimpap	비빔밥	receive [to]	받다
picture	그림; 사진	red [to be]	빨갛다
pizza	피자	red-pepper paste	고추장
place	곳; 군데; 데	refreshing [be]	시원하다
plan	계획	relationship	사이
plan [to]	계획하다	repeat after [to]	따라하다
play	연극	resemble [to]	닮다
play [to]	틀다 (music);	rest [to]	쉬다
	치다 (tennis);	restaurant	식당, 음식점
	놀다; 켜다 (violin);	restroom	화장실
	하다 (game,	return	돌려 주다;
	sports)	something [to]	돌려 드리다*hon.*
playground	운동장	return [to]	돌아오다
plural particle	들	review	복습
political science	정치학	review [to]	복습하다
population	인구	rice	밥
post office	우체국	ride [to]	타다
practice	연습	ride regularly [to]	타고 다니다
practice [to]	연습하다	right side	오른쪽
preparation	준비	ring	반지
prepare [to]	준비하다	road	길
present	선물	rock music	록
president	대통령	rock-paper-scissors	가위바위보
presidential election	대통령 선거	room	방
pretty [to be]	예쁘다	roommate	룸메이트
price	값	run [to]	뛰다
probably	아마	Russia	러시아
professor	교수님	sad [to be]	슬프다
professor's office	연구실	sale	세일
promise	약속	salesperson	점원
psychology	심리학	salty [to be]	짜다
pulgogi	불고기	sandwich	샌드위치
put forth effort	수고하다	Saturday	토요일
put on [to]	입다 (clothes)	scarce [to be]	적다
put something	놓아 주다	school	학교
down for		school vacation	방학
someone [to]		school year	학년
question	질문	season	계절
quick(ly)	어서	seat	자리
quickly	빨리	second [the]	두 번째
quiet [to be]	조용하다	see [to]	보다; 뵙다*hum.*
radio	라디오	seen [to be]	보이다

select [to]	고르다
sell [to]	팔다
semester	학기
send [to]	보내다
senior	4학년
Seol-ak Mount	설악산
Seoul	서울
service	서비스
several	여러
shirt	셔츠
shoes	신발
shop [to]	쇼핑하다
shopping	쇼핑
short [to be]	짧다; (키가) 작다
shower	샤워
sibling(s)	형제
sick [to be]	아프다
side	쪽
side [the]	옆
side dishes	반찬
sightsee [to]	구경하다
signify [to]	뜻하다
sing [to]	노래 부르다
singer	가수
sit [to]	앉다
size	사이즈
ski [to]	스키 타다
skirt	치마
sleep	잠
sleep [to]	자다; 주무시다 *hon.*
slow(ly)	천천히
small [to be]	작다 (in size)
smoke [to]	피우다
sneakers	운동화
snow	눈
snow [to]	눈(이) 오다
so	그래서
soccer	축구
socks	양말
soft tofu stew	순두부 찌개
sometimes	가끔
son	아들
song	노래
soon	금방
sophomore	2학년
sorry [to be]	미안하다; 죄송하다

sour [to be]	시다
soybean-paste stew	된장찌개
spacious [to be]	넓다
spaghetti	스파게티
Spain	스페인
speak [to]	말하다
speech	말; 말씀 *hon.*
spend time [to]	보내다
spicy [to be]	맵다
sports	스포츠
sports shoes	운동화
spot	군데
spring	봄
stairs	계단
stamp	우표
station	역
stay [to]	계시다 *hon.*
still	아직
stockings	양말
stomach	배
store	가게
straight	똑바로; 쪽
street	거리; 길
stress	스트레스
student	학생
student center	학생회관
study	공부
study [to]	공부하다
subject	과목
subject particle	이/가; 께서 *hon.*
subway	지하철
subway line	호선
suffix inserted	이
after a Korean first name that ends in a consonant	
summer	여름
Sunday	일요일
supermarket	슈퍼
sweater	스웨터
sweet [to be]	달다
swim [to]	수영하다
swimming	수영
swimming pool	수영장
switch [to]	바꾸다
switch on [to]	틀다 (music)
Sydney	시드니

table	상; 테이블	Thursday	목요일
take [to]	찍다 (a photo)	time	때; 시간
take [to]	걸리다 (time)	tired [to be]	피곤하다
take [to]	갖고 가다	to	으로
take a course	듣다	to (a person or	한테
take a shower	샤워하다	an animal)	
take off [to]	벗다	to (a person)	께 *hon.*
take something to	갖다 주다	to (destination)	에
someone [to]	갖다 드리다 *hum.*	to (time)	까지
take trouble [to]	수고하다	today	오늘
talk	이야기 (=얘기)	together	같이
talk [to]	이야기하다	Tokyo	도쿄
	(=얘기하다)	tomorrow	내일
tall [to be]	키가 크다	too (particle)	도
tasteless	맛없다	too	또
taxi	택시	too much	너무
taxi fare	택시비	tooth	이
tea	차	top side [the]	위
teach [to]	가르치다	topic particle	은/는 ('as for')
teacher	선생님	toward	으로
teacher's wife	사모님	traditional Korean	한복
telephone	전화	dress	
telephone bill	전화비	traffic	교통
telephone number	전화 번호	traffic light	신호등
television	텔레비전	train	기차
tennis	테니스	travel	여행
tennis court	테니스장	travel [to]	여행하다
test	시험	truck	트럭
textbook	교과서	truly	참
than	보다	Tuesday	화요일
thankful [to be]	감사하다; 고맙다	tuition fees	학비
that	그	turn [to]	돌다
that (over there)	저	turn into [to]	되다
then [(if so)]	그럼	turn on [to]	틀다 (music)
there	거기	two	둘
therefore	그래서	two	두 (with counter)
these days	요즘	Tylenol	타이레놀
thing	거 (= 것)	uh	저어
thirsty [to be]	목(이) 마르다	umbrella	우산
this	이	uncle	큰아버지 (father's
this	이거 (=이것)		older brother)
this time	이번	uncomfortable	불편하다
this way	이쪽으로	[to be]	
this year	올해	undesirable [to be]	싫다
thread	실	unfold [to]	펴다
thriller	스릴러	uninteresting [to be]	재미없다
through	까지 (time)	Union Building	유니온 빌딩

United Kingdom	영국	well [to be]	안녕하다
United States	미국	Western-style	양식 (food)
university	대학; 대학교	what	몇
until	까지 (time)	what	무슨
upright	똑바로	what	무엇 (=뭐)
up to	까지 (location)	what kind of	무슨; 어떤
us	우리; 저희 *hum.*	what's the matter	웬일
use [to]	쓰다	what place	어디
usually	보통	when	언제
Vancouver	밴쿠버	where	어디
very	아주	which	어느
very much	굉장히; 무척	which	어떤
vicinity	근처	white [to be]	하얗다
violin	바이올린	who	누구
visible [to be]	보이다	who	누가 (누구+가)
voice	목소리	why	왜
volume	권 (counter)	wide [to be]	넓다
wait [to]	기다리다	win [to]	이기다
walk [to]	걷다	winter	겨울
walk regularly [to]	걸어다니다	with	하고
want to [to]	싶다	without any	그냥
warm [to be]	따뜻하다	special reason	
wash [to]	빨래하다	without doing	그만
	(laundry)	anything further	
wash [to]	설거지하다	woman	여자
	(dishes)	won	원 (Korean
wash [to]	세수하다 (face)		currency)
wash [to]	손(을) 씻다	words	말; 말씀 *hon.*
	(hands)	work	일
watch	시계	work [to]	일하다
watch [to]	보다	work [to not]	놀다
water	물	World Cup	월드컵
we	우리; 저희 *hum.*	write [to]	쓰다
wealthy person	부자	year	년 (counter)
wear [to]	끼다 (glasses,	years old	살 (counter)
	gloves, rings)	yellow [to be]	노랗다
wear [to]	신다 (footwear)	yes	네 (=예)
wear [to]	쓰다 (headgear)	yesterday	어제
wear [to]	입다 (clothes)	yet	아직
weather	날씨	you	너
Wednesday	수요일	young [to be]	어리다
week	주	younger brother	남동생
weekend	주말	younger sibling	동생
well	잘	younger sister	여동생
Well; It's hard to	글쎄요	youngest child	막내
say.			